D1050324

Dead For Nothing? by Phil Pringle
Published by PaX Ministries Pty Ltd ABN No: 97 003 162 392
Locked Bag No 8, Dee Why, 2099, Australia
Tel: +61 2 9972 8688 Fax: +61 2 9972 8640
www.ccc.org.au/pax

Cover Design and Layout by Velvet Creative
www.velvet.com.au

Cover image 'Cross' by Phil Pringle
Acrylic on card.125mm x 170mm
Similar cards available at
'The Gallery' on +61 29972 8688

Printed in Australia by Southwood Press Pty Ltd
www.southwoodpress.com.au

This book or parts thereof may not be reproduced in any form, stored in a retrieval system, or transmitted in any form by any means - electronic, mechanical, photocopy, recording, or otherwise - without prior written permission of the publisher, except as provided by Australian copyright law.

Scripture taken from THE MESSAGE. Copyright © 1993, 1994, 1995, 1996, 2000, 2001, 2002. Used by permission of NavPress Publishing Group.

Scripture taken from the New King James version. Copyright © 1979, 1980, 1982. By Thomas Nelson, Inc. Used by permission. All rights reserved.

Scripture taken from the HOLY BIBLE, NEW INTERNATIONAL VERSION. Copyright © 1973, 1978, 1984 by International Bible Society. Used by permission of Zondervan Publishing House.

Scripture quotations are taken from The Living Bible, copyright ©1971. Used by permission of Tyndale House Publishers, Inc., Wheaton, IL 60189 USA. All rights reserved.

Words in capitals, in bold or in scripture quotations are the emphasis of the author. The words "him", "his", "he", or "man" are sometimes used generically to describe people of both genders.

Copyright 2003 by Pax Ministries Pty Ltd. All Rights Reserved
International Standard Book No (ISBN) 0 9585827 2 6

DEAD FOR NOTHING?

WHAT THE CROSS HAS DONE FOR YOU

PHIL PRINGLE

CONTENTS

1. Salvation 1

2. Set Free From Sin 7

3. Set Free From Sickness 23
   Laying on of hands 33
   The gift of healing 37
   People are healed as others join together and pray for them 38
   The Word of God heals people 40

4. Set Free From The Devil 43

5. Set Free From Poverty 51

6. Set Free From The Curse Of The Law 67

7. Set Free From Self 91

8. Set Free From The World 107

9. Speak The Word 119

FOREWORD

Back to the cross! We've all heard the message or we've read an article along these lines at sometime. "Back to the cross." It's a good call, saying we are distant from the cross. We need to make the journey back. The cross is central to our Christianity. Yet I can't help feeling that the "getting back to the cross" message is presented as a morbid, solemn experience of deep reflection, remorse and sorrow. Of course this is important when we need to repent and get right with God. **But repentance is a doorway. We don't live in a doorway. Faith is the living room.**

There is much more to the work of the cross than initially meets the eye. The cross presents us with the singularly most powerful and enormous work of God in the Earth. To "get back to the cross", is to get back to a life, an amazing life, based on the death and resurrection of Jesus rather than the efforts of man.

We live in a day when unprecedented numbers of people are asking Christ to come into their lives (various sources estimate about 120,000 daily). It is imperative this great harvest of souls has its roots in the Word of God. We must discover and grasp the work Jesus has accomplished on the cross.

It's amazing how many of us judge the effectiveness of the cross by what our feelings tell us. If certain feelings have failed to appear in us, we conclude it can't be true, it doesn't work, or God is not interested in us. This is wrong thinking. Actually, "the truths of salvation are appropriated by a faith that acts." This is similar to the story of the Israelites possessing the land of Canaan. The Promised Land is to be possessed, sometimes by simply walking into it, sometimes with a battle, but it must be **appropriated**.

Appropriating truth means **that we first gain understanding of what the Word has promised, then we make our emotions and thoughts line up with what God has stated.** Truth lies unattended to and unappropriated because we would rather it all just become ours without any effort. If we are waiting for our feelings to tell us whether the Word is true or not we will be disappointed. Feelings, even if positive, are still not accurate as a guide for living. But for many, this is a normal way of life. If we don't feel forgiven, but rather feel guilty, we conclude this must be the truth. We decide we are not forgiven. Why? Because we don't have the feeling of forgiveness. We still **feel** guilty. Yet the Bible has declared us **acquitted and justified!**

> **"...being justified freely by His grace through the redemption that is in Christ Jesus..."**
> Romans 3:24

We take hold of truth and make our feelings embrace it. This is where the battle is. Our mind does not easily accept truth. It would rather gain its information from the five senses than from the Word of God.

Yet Paul says we are to "pull down", **every high thought** that exalts itself against the knowledge of God (2 Cor 10:5). This means **we**, I repeat, **we**, not God, we pull down those thoughts that disagree with the Word. **We** make our mind conform to the Word of God (Rom 12:2).

We speak the Word into our thoughts. Speaking the Word of God has enormous impact on our spiritual life. It is the Sword of the Holy Spirit (Eph 6:17). It is a double-edged sword (Heb 4:12). It has a twin effect. It defeats the devil and builds our faith all in one action. Again we are told by the Apostle to "take up" our spiritual armour (Eph 6:13). It isn't placed upon us. It is clothing **we take up** and place on ourselves. The battle is won because we fight. And **we fight** with the sword of the Spirit. **The Word of God.**

This is appropriating truth. There's a lot of soap in the world. But there are still a lot of dirty people. If we don't use the soap it has no effect upon us. Truth is there. Learning to appropriate truth and live in it, is the constant pursuit for the believer.

1

SALVATION

"For Yah, the Lord, is my strength and song;
He has also become my salvation"
Isaiah 12:2,3

1

SALVATION

> **"Behold, God is my salvation, I will trust and not be afraid; 'For Yah, the Lord, is my strength and song; He also has become my salvation.' Therefore with joy you will draw water from the wells of salvation."** Isaiah 12:2,3

God has brought salvation to the Earth through Christ. This salvation came through the cross. It is called a **complete** salvation, a **perfect** salvation. Nothing can be added to it, or taken from it (Heb 7:27).

Many believers live in defeat because they haven't yet grasped the fullness of their salvation. We must realise the work of the cross has provided an absolutely complete salvation for the person who is accepting Christ.

This "so great a salvation" (Heb 2:3) encompasses deliverance from all that destroys people. God loves us. He has sent Jesus to save us from those things threatening our present wholeness and eternal well being. For some however, salvation relates only to deliverance from hell and gaining entrance to Heaven. This obviously is the awesome work of the cross, yet it is not the only work.

Old Testament believers understood salvation in terms of deliverance from oppressive enemies, destructive circumstances, diseases and disasters. Yahweh was their saviour from calamity. The Holman Bible Dictionary paints it like this: *"In the Old Testament, salvation primarily concerns God's saving acts within human history. The early prophets anticipated God's salvation to be realised in the earth's renewed fruitfulness and the rebuilding of the ruined cities of Israel. Salvation would extend to all nations who would stream to Zion for instruction in God's ways."* (Amos 9:13-15, Isa 2:2-4). The Old Testament concept also related to a community or a national salvation more than a personal, individual kind.

The view of salvation has been expanded. The New Testament salvation is the rescue from an eternal hell that awaits the wicked beyond this life. However, God's will for us in the "here and now" has not changed. He is still the deliverer. He is still the healer. He is still the provider of abundance. More specifically, God has provided these benefits through the work of Jesus on the cross. This is where we are going in this book – the seven great works of the cross.

Through the Cross we have been;

1. **Set free from sin.**
2. **Set free from sickness.**
3. **Set free from the devil.**
4. **Set free from poverty.**
5. **Set free from the curse of the law.**
6. **Set free from us.**
7. **Set free from the world.**

2

SET FREE FROM SIN

"He breaks the power of cancelled sin."

2

SET FREE FROM SIN

There is no other way to remove sin from the soul than through the blood of Jesus (1Pet 1:18). Sin separates God and people. The blood of Jesus reconciles us with God because sin is completely removed (Isa 59:2). Through the work of the blood of Jesus our stained soul is washed whiter than snow (Col 1:20). We are completely set free from sin through Christ's death. God removes all sin, all iniquities, all trespasses, and all offences. Everything keeping us from God, Jesus has removed through His blood.

The hymn writer, Charles Wesley, penned it brilliantly saying, *"He breaks the power of cancelled sin."*

> **"For sin shall not have dominion over you, for you are not under law but under grace."** Romans 6:14

The balls on a bowling green all have bias so they veer to one side. This is like sin in us. We are born with a bias toward wrong, away from God. We don't have to teach children to do wrong, to lie, and to be mischievous. It comes naturally. When we are born again this is changed so that we receive a bias towards God. As we roll through life we lean towards doing right, towards God.

Sin is the basis of all our problems. Yet, ignoring this fact, we seek solutions to these problems through a thousand other ways. If we fail to deal properly with sin we will only ever continue struggling with these unsolved problems.

When we repent from sin and accept Christ, sin is erased from our soul, from our record before God, and from His memory. He declares,

> **"I, even I, am He who blots out your transgressions for My own sake; and I will not remember your sins."** Isaiah 43:25

It is a natural instinct for us to attempt to get right with God through our own effort. We feel that if we are just good enough, our sins will be atoned for or at least overlooked and we will be right with God. This kind of thinking may pacify our conscience. But our conscience is not God. Being right with God in Heaven is an enormously different affair. Jesus has died for us because **our good works cannot save us** or get us into a right relationship with God. We hear the term, "fallen from grace", applied to someone once considered a godly person who has stumbled into an immoral lifestyle. Yet that Scripture actually applies to those who have reverted to trying to gain salvation through their own effort rather than relying upon the work of Jesus to secure righteousness for them.

> **"You have become estranged from Christ, you who attempt to be justified by law; you have fallen from grace."** Galatians 5:4

Today, we are so unwilling to deal with "facing the music" we desperately seek to remove the responsibility for our wrongdoing from ourselves. Whilst stopping short of "the devil made me do it", we are really just saying exactly that in a more sophisticated manner. "Dysfunctional behaviour" is blamed on everything else but ourselves. "It's my genetic coding", or "the environment I was raised in", or "the way my grandmother treated my mother and then the way she treated me", or "the tragedies I experienced as a child", or "pressure of the situation I was in", or "I was so influenced by another person I can't be held responsible for my actions!"

These arguments are all very convenient until we ourselves are the mother or the father being blamed for the misdemeanours of our offspring. In the Old Testament, if children committed serious crimes they could be stoned. Today if children play up, we stone the parents! And the parents' stone themselves, because they believe that the behaviour of their children is totally a result of how they have been raised. Every one of us is born with the propensity to sin. It's deep within our nature to want to do wrong, and then to do it. It takes a change of heart by the power of the Holy Spirit to make this any different.

The only way to deal with sin is to repent from it and then be cleansed through the blood of Christ. It is increasingly popular to think of wrongdoing as a dysfunction or an "illness" of the person committing the wrongdoing. Criminals are often looked on with pity even though they have committed terrible atrocities. "There's something faulty with the poor boy." The victims become short changed on compassion and feel justice has not been done. Authorities speak of rehabilitation and healing, and counselling. It is a virtue to extend pity and compassion but this cannot be done at the exclusion of justice. Some of the best rehabilitative processes are to make people face their crime, and then accept the penalty due. If justice is "fallen", a deep cynicism about life develops in the minds of the community. When people feel that life is unfair they develop deep frustrations. The inevitable consequence of frustration is anger and violence.

When we wrongly diagnose our problems we prescribe the wrong answers.

Sin is not sickness. It cannot be healed. Many people have been treated badly in their early, developing years. Some have been abused, others ignored and abandoned, whilst others have been smothered by over-protective parents. All kinds of influences are at work in our lives. However, to **explain** why we behave badly doesn't **excuse** us. An explanation is neither an excuse nor a justification for evildoing. We still have the power of choice. We do make decisions as to how we will respond to those events of our life. We will not be standing before the throne of God on Judgement Day and be able to neatly skirt around the things we did by declaring, "It wasn't my fault, my genes made me do it."

Even if we were somehow out of control at some stage and did things that were wrong, we must accept responsibility for the fact that it was us who did it. This is the only way to rid ourselves of the impulse of sin within. It is not a sickness—it is sin.

Sin is a force we are born with. It drives us to do things that are wrong and offensive to God and man. The only way to deal with this force is through repentance and the blood of Jesus Christ. Repentance begins by accepting the responsibility for our actions, then confessing it to the Father. If we don't accept responsibility for our actions we will not be set free from the problem. It will recur. Once sin is dealt with, everything that gains a hold on our lives through sin is disabled. Sickness, demon possession and curses are a result of sin. When the foundation for their existence is gone, they can be dealt with properly.

To repent is to accept responsibility for our actions. Our flesh does not want to do this. It's the devil that diverts us. Well meaning friends try to relieve us from accepting the responsibility for our own behaviour, but we must come into the light.

> **"For everyone practicing evil hates the light and does not come to the light, lest his deeds should be exposed. But he who does the truth comes to the light, that his deeds may be clearly seen, that they have been done in God."** John 3:20,21

This is the first basic truth which is fundamental to the Christian life, if this does not happen when we are new believers, we will never find ourselves able to live a powerful Christian life. Life itself demands we face uncomfortable situations. If we never gain the ability to come into the light, to be honest about ourselves and surrounding situations, we will never build a great and successful life for God. A basic premise for success in life is that we face difficult circumstances—emotionally uncomfortable and conflicting encounters. Repentance is when we first learn to do this. It's uncomfortable to admit guilt, to not shift the blame, to accept full responsibility and to accept shame. **Repentance is taking sides with God against ourselves.** When we do this we have found the key to freedom.

When we fail to accept responsibility for our actions, we inadvertently lose control of our lives. Although it is convenient to avoid the unpleasant emotional confrontation by saying we were not really in control of our behaviour, but it is in that process that we surrender control. If we take our hands off the wheel regarding our past, then we have also taken our hands off the wheel for our present and future. It's the same wheel. Our past and our present obviously powerfully influence our future.

Authority is inextricably entwined with responsibility. When we deny that we had any choice about our actions in the past, that we had no control, no authority, we surrender the most priceless gift God has given us; the power of free will, the power of choice and the authority to make decisions. The more we refuse to accept that we have this right, the more we reinforce our inability to take authority over our future.

We must understand that God has already created an environment of forgiveness and mercy.

> "**...God was in Christ reconciling the world to Himself, not imputing their trespasses to them.**" 2 Corinthians 5:19

When Jesus was dying on the cross, He was not condemning the world but bringing forgiveness and salvation to the world. He was not imputing our trespasses to us. He was reconciling you and I to God.

When the prodigal son returns home we, read in Luke 15:20 that the Father was running to meet him. Now, take into consideration that the father's reputation had been seriously maligned through his son's behaviour. He had also been left short handed on the farm. Also, at least one third of his life's savings had been squandered by his renegade boy. His own feelings of disappointment over the boy were high. His remorse over his own ability as a parent plagued him.

Given all this, it was perfectly reasonable for the prodigal to expect that the man running towards him was anything but merciful. He was expecting his father to pull a shotgun out of his back pocket and begin firing. But the Father kept running, not producing a weapon of any kind. He just outstretched his arms—outstretched and embracing. The father hugged and kissed the boy. Immediately the boy repented, accepting full responsibility for his actions, begging to be received back into the family as a servant. The father promptly restored him to full sonship with all its privileges.

If the father had come with a gun, or worse, a pointing, accusing, shaking finger; the son would have given a repentance that did not fully engage the heart. When we say sorry to someone who is condemning us already, it is normal that they still carry on with their accusations even after we have confessed and have offered apologies. So we eventually say something petulant like, "Well, I said I'm sorry; take it or leave it!" This is not repentance. God has provided a "safe" environment of mercy, with forgiveness already given, for us to repent in.

Forgiveness is one of the greatest luxuries of life. To experience forgiveness and acceptance by the Father is enormous. The word forgiveness (Greek–"aphiemi"), means "to loose, to set away, to set free." Many of us fail to experience the forgiveness of God because we do not forgive ourselves. **God moves in our moving.** Once aware of the will of God, I then implement it. We can give mental assent to a truth without letting it touch our lives at all. We must enact the Word of God. If we hear and fail to do then our "religion is in vain", (James 1:22). When we stop roasting ourselves for past failures and forgive ourselves we experience the forgiveness of God entering our lives. We will also find it easier to forgive others, once we have learned to forgive ourselves.

Forgiveness is the way of God because it accepts we have done wrong, we have violated a high moral expectation on ourselves but that there is mercy. Forgiveness doesn't justify a bad action, or excuse it. Rather, when we seek forgiveness we find mercy.

This merciful attitude must be in our own soul towards ourselves. Once the wall of self judgment is broken the bridge of forgiveness to ourselves is erected. God's forgiveness flows easily into our inner world, so that we feel the forgiveness of God. This obviously affects so many other areas.

If we live in a self-loathing we will not be happy with ourselves or others, although we may acknowledge the theory that God loves us. That's all it can be; a theory—because we can't feel a thing! Once we forgive ourselves though we can move on to accepting ourselves and even liking, or, loving ourselves. Then we can feel worth. We can accept the worth God has placed upon us. This state of healthy self image is a platform for God. He will speak words of comfort and encouragement to us constantly throughout our lives, but when we actually apply these things to ourselves by the doing of it to ourselves, it releases the power of God to make His truths live in us. God rarely forces Himself upon us. He moves through our movings.

People need to be told not to be so hard on themselves. If God is prepared to forgive you, why can't you forgive you? Go ahead and tell yourself that you forgive yourself, just like God has forgiven you. Say it!

"I forgive myself. I will not hold my sins against myself any longer! Thank you Lord for helping me forgive myself. Thank you for forgiving me. I accept it fully. Amen."

Guilt is one of the worst effects of sin. Our emotions are not built to carry guilt. Under the pressure of guilt we find ourselves doing things wrong, and doing wrong things. When we feel uncomfortable within because of guilt, and are preoccupied with the sense of wrong; everybody and everything else is an intrusion into our world. We react wrongly to people and events around us. Guilt dissolves as we accept forgiveness and cleansing from God.

The world attempts to remove guilt by legitimising the wrong we did in the first place. It has long been a ploy of our fallen nature, to escape repentance and the need to forsake doing wrong. Repentance not only involves accepting responsibility for our actions and confessing our sin to the Lord, but also forsaking the wrong.

> **"He who covers his sins will not prosper, but whoever confesses and forsakes them will have mercy."** Proverbs 28:13

Besides telling us that we will never be successful if we cover our sins, this Scripture calls on us not to just confess our sins, but also to abandon them; to stop doing them. If we determine inside to turn from doing those things, God's power will accompany us in the effort.

Part of the process of making the decision to no longer continue in sin, is to actually correct our past. Repentance also involves making right what is wrong. This is foundational to building strength of character. It is the basis of integrity. No one will live a perfect life. When we do fall, we must be prepared to "face the music" as it were, and put things right. This is challenging, difficult and uncomfortable, but if we are to walk in the light we must be committed to this.

Restitution should take place within the circle of offence. If I have offended a person then I need to make it right with them. It is not necessary for me to confess my failure to anyone else. If I have had critical thoughts or bad attitudes towards others, then I need to confess that only to God Himself. If the people concerned are unaware of my difficulties it is only an added burden to their life for me to load them up with my problems. Stolen goods should be returned. Zacchaeus returned four times more than he wrongly took from his own people (Luke 19:8). His sense of making his wrongs right was strong, and he was determined to please God.

Whatever it means to put things right, we should do it. It may mean writing a letter of apology, straightening crooked business practices or admitting to lies or cheating. All these things lay a foundation for a powerful, immovable life. This is a very truth for some, but without it we build a house that will fall when the storms come. A clear conscience is the secret to a bold life. When there are no skeletons in the closet we are not checking over our shoulder for the rest of our days.

God moves in our moving. Once our will is set in motion we can expect the power of God to assist us. Even though we may slip and fall in this pursuit of forsaking sin, the blood of Christ is still effective to cleanse us.

> "**Though he fall, he shall not be utterly cast down; for the Lord upholds him with His hand.**" Psalm 37:24

God fully understands our flesh, and our propensity towards sin, so He has made provision for this in the New Covenant.

> **"If we confess our sins, He is faithful and just to forgive us our sins and to cleanse us from all unrighteousness."** 1 John 1:9

The blood of Christ is not just effective when we first come to Christ and receive salvation. We will need it many times throughout our Christian life. Even though we may feel disappointed with ourselves we are not to run from God when we fall, but run to Him.

When He attempted to wash Peter's feet (John 13:10), Jesus told Peter that although he was completely washed He still needed to wash his hands and feet. The picture Jesus was creating for the disciples refers to the Roman public baths. People would wash in the public baths and then return home. On the way however, their feet and their hands would become dirty again. So, arriving at home they wash their hands and feet. This is the Christian walk. We first meet Christ and He washes us completely clean. We receive salvation and acceptance into the family of God.

As we travel through our lives though, there will be times when we offend God (1 John 1:8). At these points we must repent, confess, and turn from our offences again. We are promised the blood of Jesus will cleanse us again so that sin and all the curses that come with it will not stick to our lives (1 John 1:9).

This is the great work of the cross. God, through grace has provided a means for regular cleansing, and renewing of our relationship with the Lord. Thus the power of the Cross is manifested in our life. Repentance is how we apply the blood of Christ to our soul and so find the power of cleansing and forgiveness through the blood of the Lamb.

In Romans 6:14, Paul tells us that ***"sin will no longer have dominion over us"***. This is because the force of sin has been destroyed in Christ. The impulse of sin, the motivation towards evil has been destroyed through the cross. Jesus has not only forgiven us for the sins we have committed but He has also provided a death to sin itself. He actually became sin for us (2 Cor 5:21) and then put that force to death, so whoever receives Christ receives the death of sin in their lives and the power of righteousness.

3

SET FREE FROM SICKNESS

"If Jesus has borne our sicknesses
then we no longer need to."

3

SET FREE FROM SICKNESS

"...who Himself bore our sins in His own body on the tree, that we, having died to sins, might live for righteousness; by whose stripes you were healed." 1 Peter 2:24

"For his wounds have healed ours!" TLB

Jesus has taken our sicknesses upon Himself so that we do not have to bear them on ourselves.

"...that it might be fulfilled which was spoken by Isaiah the prophet, saying: 'He Himself took our infirmities and bore our sicknesses.'" Matthew 8:17

If Jesus has borne our sicknesses then we no longer need to.

Healing is ours through the work of the cross. The Cross is the basis for wholeness. When Jesus took our sins away, He also took our diseases away.

Since the Book of Genesis God has revealed Himself as the ultimate healer. When He manifested in the flesh as Jesus, it was only completely in keeping with His Divine nature to heal sickness. It has always been the will of God to heal sickness. Whenever He sees sickness, it's His nature to heal it.

He revealed Himself as the healer of Israel through His name **Jehovah Rapha**—"The Lord who heals you" (Exo 15:26).

The Lord established the fact that if they would destroy the false gods of the surrounding nations and serve Jehovah exclusively, then He would ensure sickness was removed from their lives.

> "**...I will take sickness away from the midst of you.**" Exodus 23:25

Throughout the Old Testament, time and time again, healing comes with the Atonement, Intercession and the Passover sacrifices.

In Genesis 20:17 Abraham intercedes for the house of Abimilech and all the women are healed of barrenness.

When Israel left Egypt they sacrificed a lamb for each household. After this, there was not one sick one among them as they marched out of bondage (Psa 105:37).

When they were bitten by a plague of snakes in the desert, Moses lifted up a brass likeness of the snake on a pole, and anyone who looked at it was healed (Num 21v8,9). Jesus Himself referred to this as being exactly what was to happen to Him (John 3:14). That He would be lifted up. It also follows, that whoever looks to the cross will discover healing.

In Leviticus 14 we read of the priests placing the blood of a sacrifice on the leper and once the ceremony was complete the leper was cleansed. Healing took place as the person received the blood of the sacrifice. Leprosy has always been a symbol of sin. The cleansing of the leprosy is a symbol of the cleansing of sin, plus it demonstrates actual healing of the disease as well.

When Hezekiah kept the Passover in 2 Chronicles 30:20, ***"...the Lord listened to Hezekiah and healed the people."***

In 1 Corinthians 11:30, Paul tells the believers they are weak and sickly, because they have failed to correctly estimate the Lord's body. Some were taking of it unworthily, because of attitudes and a lifestyle that were unacceptable to the Lord. But there were others also who were sick and failing to appropriate the work of the cross into their lives.

All of these events tell us that **healing and the atonement are connected.**

Through the fall we lost everything. Through the Cross, Jesus recovered everything. The salvation of any part of man without sacrifice, without the shedding of blood, is unknown in Scripture.

Dr Young, author of 'Youngs Analytical Concordance' translates Isaiah 53:4 as, *"Surely our sickness (Hebrew – "choli") He has borne, and our pains He has carried them…and by His bruise there is healing for us."*

Dr. Isaac Leeser, translator of the Hebrew English Bible, renders these verses as, *"He was despised and shunned by men; A man of pains and acquainted with disease. But only our diseases did He bear Himself, and our pains He carried."*

When Jesus was crucified He was dealing with more than just sin. He was providing the basis for healing, and delivering people from sickness. Many times the two actions are placed side by side. The Psalmist declares;

> "**(The Lord)…Who forgives all your iniquities, Who heals all your diseases…**" Psalm 103:3

In the forgiveness of sin there is also the healing of diseases. God is not limited to forgiving only a few select sins. He forgives ALL sins. The same applies to disease. He heals ALL diseases. There is no disease God is incapable of healing. **Jesus saw little difference in setting a person free from their sin and setting them free from their sickness.**

> **"For which is easier, to say, 'Your sins are forgiven you,' or to say, 'Arise and walk? But that you may know that the Son of Man has power on earth to forgive sins'; then He said to the paralytic, 'Arise, take up your bed, and go to your house.'"** Matthew 9:5,6

The man was immediately healed. Jesus declared that healing and forgiveness of sin work together.

To discover the power of the cross for healing I must understand how to appropriate truth. If it was a meal on a plate I could eat it. If it was an item in a store we could purchase it. If it was a fruit on a tree we could pluck it. Even though these may serve well as spiritual metaphors, the truth is we are always in need of knowing how to make spiritual truths physical realities in our world. The bridge between the two is always faith. **Faith makes real the promises of God.**

Faith is released because it is fully confident it is in the will of God. Healing has always been, is, and always will be the will of God. He never changes. He's the same yesterday, today and forever (Heb 13:8). Jesus was the express image of God in the Earth (Heb 1:3). He is the perfect revelation of the will of God. He is the character of God manifested on planet Earth.

Not once do we find Jesus laying His hands on anyone to make them sick. The suggestion verges on blasphemy. He only ever healed the sick. Acts 10:38 tells us that it is the devil who damages people, and Jesus who makes them whole. When Jesus was asked if he would heal sick people, His answer was, "Yes!" (Mat 8:2,3). He is no respecter of persons (Acts 10:34). What He has done for others, He will do for you and me. All who came to Him, He healed (Mat 8:16). Few doubt His ability to heal. But many are uncertain of His willingness to heal them. If He has healed others, why would He not heal you and me? We are neither better nor worse than those God has touched in other times.

Faith always starts with desire. We want something to happen. Faith always wants a thing strong enough to do whatever it takes. Faith begins with a desire strong enough to make you determined to make it happen. There is more.

Faith decides it will get it. Faith is determined. It makes it's mind up. It is not double minded. The decision is made. I'm going to get healed. I don't entertain "But what if?" The decision is made. We're committed.

Faith asks God to make it happen. Faith cries out to God no matter what pressures there are to block us. Faith persists. It doesn't give up because of a few disappointments. It keeps on asking. It does not allow it's heart to be discouraged. Discouragement is one of the worst enemies of faith. It is imperative to rise above every rejection and persevere until the answer is there.

Faith is certain of a miracle. It knows God is involved. It doesn't pretend. Faith is an inward clear knowledge and revelation of realities that are not evident to the natural senses. Faith is so certain of those realities that it acts as though they are true; simply because they are. It makes decisions based on those certainties. It plans according to what faith knows.

Faith speaks of those realities as finished acts. It says, "Thank You Lord. It's already done." "It's already happened", "I've got it right now", "God has done it." Faith always speaks. It's the first reaction faith has. If we believe a thing we speak it. It's not necessarily loud, because it's not relying on volume, or excitement, but on the power of God's Word. Faith judges God as faithful. Faith speaks the promises of God and refuses to speak those things that oppose the promises. Faith acknowledges truth rather than facts. It connects the promises with the desires of the heart. Faith gives glory to God for things not yet manifested. Faith knows it builds in the spirit first, then it falls into the natural. Faith is a creative force; that's why it speaks as God does when He creates. The Word of the Lord and healing go together. He created the worlds through His Word. Speak the Word.

Faith sees realities not seen by natural eyes. It can see the healing already happened. It can feel the emotions of the experience, because it's there, in the future, in full view of the realities of the answer. Faith spends time meditating on that vision. It does not imagine disaster, it sees the answer.

Faith acts. Without action faith is dead. Real faith always acts. Faith does not care what obstacles there are, it will surmount them to receive the answer. Four men lift the roof to lower their friend into the presence of Jesus. The paralysed man is healed. Bartimaeus, ignores the crowd trying to silence his cry for help. Jesus hears him; calls him and heals him. The Canaanite woman presses through the apparent reluctance of Jesus to heal her daughter. The disciples have pushed her back, Jesus has first ignored her, then told her she doesn't qualify for a miracle, (she is a foreigner to Israel). She keeps coming in spite of all this. She gets the miracle.

In just the same way the Father has provided forgiveness for His children, so He has provided healing for all. God has arranged for this healing to travel into our lives through several different means. Even though The Lord employs a variety of ways to impart healing, it is always based on two things. Initially healing has been secured for us through the death of Christ on the cross. Secondly faith is always essential to the equation. Faith is the currency of heaven. Faith in the person praying, faith in the sufferer, or faith expressed by others releases the power of God bringing healing to sickness.

LAYING ON OF HANDS

Healing is imparted through the laying on of hands.

> "**...they will lay hands on the sick, and they will recover.**" Mark 16:18

Through the laying on of hands God is imparted into people. Healing from God is a supernatural flow of the life of God. Healing is spiritual life. This "life" is not nothing. We must understand that God is not nothing. God is something. God is spirit, and spirit is something.

> "**God is Spirit...**" John 4:24

For want of a better term, God is stuff. Spirit is not nothing. Spirit is something. Spirit is a substance albeit a spiritual one. Spirit substance cannot be seen with physical eyes, felt with our physical body, heard with physical ears, or smelled or tasted with our nose or mouth. Our physical bodies are not equipped to contact spiritual realms. Spirit relates to spirit. Flesh relates to flesh.

> "**That which is born of the flesh is flesh, and that which is born of the Spirit is spirit.**" John 3:6

> "**For those who live according to the flesh set their minds on the things of the flesh, but those who live according to the Spirit, the things of the Spirit.**" Romans 8:5

However, we are spiritual beings. Our spiritual nature finds expression through our physical bodies. We are "temples" (1 Cor 3:16) of the Holy Spirit. Our own spirit lives within us (Dan 7:15). The Father and Jesus dwell within us (John 14:23). These are all spirit entities. Spiritual life can be imparted from one person to another, from one thing to another. This happens through the laying on of hands. This applies to many more areas than just healing. However, healing is a primary application of the laying on of hands. The "stuff" of God travels from one person to another through the laying on of hands. This "stuff" can actually permeate physical things. Spiritual life can get inside physical things.

Paul laid his hands on cloth and when it was laid on sick people, whatever had gotten into the cloth was released into the sufferers body, and they were healed.

> "**...so that even handkerchiefs or aprons were brought from his body to the sick, and the diseases left them and the evil spirits went out of them.**" Acts 19:12

This miraculous power lives inside the physical body. We sometimes imagine that because spirit is not physical that it is somehow separate from our body. We imagine that we are a hollow case, and that our spirit dwells in the hollow. This is not the case at all. The spiritual life of God actually infuses the physical body. This life of God gets inside our flesh and our bones. This is where the healing life of God, the "stuff" of God Himself lives.

Some time after Elisha the miracle-working prophet was dead and buried, bands of Moab raiders invaded Israel.

During one of the battles, the soldiers were attempting to bury one of their fellows but the raiders attacked them. In their haste the soldiers threw the dead man into the tomb of Elisha. The bones of the prophet had become exposed. As soon as the dead man landed on the bones of Elisha, he revived. He was resurrected by the power of God still resident in the bones of a dead man who once worked miracles through the power of God.

> **"So it was, as they were burying a man, that suddenly they spied a band of raiders; and they put the man in the tomb of Elisha; and when the man was let down and touched the bones of Elisha, he revived and stood on his feet."**
> 2 Kings 13:21

The power of God lives in our flesh and bones. It lives in physical things. The presence of God permeates buildings and atmospheres. It infuses into our bodies, and our workplaces. This "stuff" of God gets into things and works miracles; changes lives, heals sicknesses, and causes evil spirits to leave. It is the Spirit of God. No evil spirit can remain as the power of God and the Holy Spirit take up residence. Light comes. Darkness goes.

This "stuff" is imparted through the laying on of hands. It travels from one person to another as we lay hands with that purpose in mind. It flows through the spiritual atmosphere of faith. It seems to matter little as to who actually is expressing that faith.

It can be the friends or relatives of a sufferer;

> **"Then behold, they brought to Him a paralytic lying on a bed. When Jesus saw their faith, He said to the paralytic, 'Son, be of good cheer; your sins are forgiven you.' "** Matthew 9:2

> **"While He spoke these things to them, behold, a ruler came and worshiped Him, saying, 'My daughter has just died, but come and lay Your hand on her and she will live.' "** Matthew 9:18

It can be the faith of the sufferer themselves;

> **"Then He touched their eyes, saying, 'According to your faith let it be to you.'"** Matthew 9:29

It can be the faith of the minister of the healing;

> **"Then Jesus answered and said, 'O faithless and perverse generation, how long shall I be with you? How long shall I bear with you? Bring him here to Me.' "** Matthew 17:17

If faith is absent and there is an active atmosphere of unbelief this severely restricts the release and flow of this life of God. Even Jesus Himself finds restrictions to the level of power released when unbelief prevails.

> **"Now He could do no mighty work there, except that He laid His hands on a few sick people and healed them...and He marvelled because of their unbelief."** Mark 6:5

THE GIFT OF HEALING

> **"...to another (is given) gifts of healings by the same Spirit..."** 1 Corinthians 12:8

Some people in the Church are especially gifted by the Holy Spirit to impart healing. They have a gift to heal sick people. All Christians can pray with an expectation for people to be healed (James 5:16), but there are definitely certain people gifted by God to minister healing to the sick. This gift is also their calling and motivation. They approach the entire Gospel from the aspect of healing. The revelation and insight these people have travels down the line of healing sicknesses. Again this gift is generally imparted through the laying on of hands.

Because there are so many kinds of sicknesses it seems that God gives people giftings that heal certain diseases in particular. This arouses higher levels of faith for people with those particular sicknesses. 1 Corinthians 12:8 speaks of the healing gifts in plural terms.

PEOPLE ARE HEALED AS OTHERS JOIN TOGETHER AND PRAY FOR THEM

> **"Confess your trespasses to one another, and pray for one another, that you may be healed. The effective, fervent prayer of a righteous man avails much."** James 5:16

When we pray for others we are interceding. We are standing in the gap. We are taking their problem on as though it was ours. We are standing before God on their behalf. Intercession gets results. As we pray fervently and effectively for one another we bring healing to the church.

As a young assistant minister, a young boy suffering around 24 epileptic fits every day was brought to me. The parents expected healing. He was becoming cut, bruised and badly damaged. I felt so sorry for the young kid and his parents who were great people. The pressure on them was becoming unbearable. I take the matter to our mid-week meeting. We join hands around the auditorium and begin praying. A great spirit of prayer comes upon us. We rise into a realm of prayer and intercession I have never experienced before.

After a little while it seems we have prayed long enough. A general feeling of rest from crying out to God comes through the room. However, the Lord says to me, "Rise again. You're not through yet." So I tell the people to rest for a few moments and then we rise again in prayer. Again, after a while the stamina of the people begins to flag. This is only after about ten minutes of this kind of prayer. Intercessory prayer is very exacting. The spiritual stamina of most people in prayer is not great. Even in worship most people can hold the position for about five minutes. Their spirit tires and they lose emotional and mental focus. I still felt we had not yet "broken through." We sang a quiet song in worship, strengthening our spirit and then prayed a third time. This time as we reached a crescendo there was a definite "crack" in the spirit. We broke through. People were clapping, shouting, jumping up and down. We had a deep witness something powerful had happened. I rang the parents of the young boy the next day. They told me he only had 4 fits that day. The next day he had none at all.

Healing travels through prayer.

THE WORD OF GOD HEALS PEOPLE

"He sent His word and healed them…"
Psalm 107:20

In the Gospels often Jesus does not go to the sufferer, but rather simply speaks the Word and the miracle happens. (Mat 8:4). As people believe the Word, healing enters their lives, or to the one they are bringing to the Lord.

A friend of mine is diagnosed with cancer. It's about the size of an orange under his ribs and under his arm. His wife doesn't allow anyone to speak anything negative anywhere in his room. She doesn't allow anyone she thinks will be speaking negative things to visit him. They plaster the walls of his hospital room with Scripture, and begin speaking the Word of God day and night. When he is finally operated on, they find the cancer, completely dead. Instead of him dying the cancer does. Jesus lives and so do those who believe Him. He heals. He works miracles. So do those who believe Him.

I have a list of Scriptures I often give people called prescription promises. The power of the Word of God is severely underestimated. The prophets Elijah and Elisha simply speak the Word of God and one after another, awesome miracles take place. Jesus speaks the Word time and again to impossible situations. This carries healing and miracles into people's lives.

The Word of God is a miracle working healing force in the Earth.

> **"For they are life to those who find them, and health to all their flesh."** Proverbs 4:22

Revelation of the Word of God is the Word being unpacked into our spirit. Revelation is light. It is truth entering our inner man. Revelation is the food of the spirit. Revelation of the Word of God is an actual life force that travels into our spirit and can be imparted through speaking it. The Word of God is a creative force. God created all that is, with His Word. The power of His Word has not been relaxed one iota. The same power is active in His Word now as was in His Word at the creation of the Earth and the entire Universe. When the Word enters our spirit, it comes as light. It is power that can be imparted. It is "stuff", that can be sent into people's bodies and situations and it brings miracles and solutions. It is the life of God.

4

SET FREE FROM THE DEVIL

"...that at the name of Jesus every knee should bow, of those in heaven, and of those on earth, and of those under the earth..."
Philippians 2:10

4

SET FREE FROM THE DEVIL

How many Christians constantly complain about the devil doing things in their lives? They seem to be completely overrun by devils attacking them all the time. This is not the position of a New Testament believer. Paul tells us we've been set free from the devil through the work of the cross.

> **"Having disarmed principalities and powers, He made a public spectacle of them, triumphing over them in it."** Colossians 2:15

This refers to the fact that Jesus has defeated the devil, in hell, and publicly displayed this fact to every demon in the realms of darkness. The conflict Jesus had with the devil was predicted right from the start in the Garden of Eden.

> "...**and I will put enmity between you and the woman, and between your seed and her seed; He shall bruise your head, and you shall bruise His heel.**" Genesis 3:15

This prophecy declared there was to be a battle where the devil would bruise the heel of Jesus, but Jesus would bruise the head of Satan. This means Jesus brought His heel down heavily on the head of the devil. For that to happen the devil had to be on the ground, defeated in a battle.

David also prophesied that Jesus would take captives in His ascension from the grave.

> "**When you ascended on high, you led captives in your train...**" Psalm 68:18

Isaiah also predicted the battle Jesus has to have and that the spoils of His victory would be shared.

> "**Therefore I will give Him a portion among the great, and He will divide the spoils with the strong, because He poured out His life unto death, and was numbered with the transgressors. For He bore the sin of many, and made intercession for the transgressors.**" Isaiah 53:12

Jesus Himself revealed the principle by which He releases people from the grip of Satan. He will first bind the devil, then He will take those who have been held captive.

> **"Or again, how can anyone enter a strong man's house and carry off his possessions unless he first ties up the strong man? Then he can rob his house."** Matthew 12:29
>
> **"But when someone stronger attacks and overpowers him, he takes away the armour in which the man trusted and divides up the spoils."** Luke 11:22

Jesus realised he had to both bind the "strongman", as well as remove all the armoury before He could take his possessions.

When Jesus died, He first went to the presence of God, then went into the regions of hell where He entered into a conflict with the devil (Luke 23:46, Eccl 12:7, 1Pet 3:19, Rev 1:18). When Peter says that Jesus "preached" to the spirits, the word used ("kerusso"), means to herald as a Public Crier. This was the person who announced news that affected everyone in a town. A trumpeter sounded to gain the attention of the people, then a royal proclamation, or whatever else, would be shouted out by the town crier. In the absence of radio, television, fax, telephone, computers, this was the only method of speaking to a large number of people at any given time.

After Jesus defeated Satan in an enormous battle in hell, He made a spectacle of the devil to all the demons and angels. He paraded the devil defeated, bound, hobbled and stripped of authority. He led the devil past all the cohorts of the evil one in the corridors of Hades.

Then Jesus announced to all the devils in hell that He now held the keys to hell and death, and that whenever any demon heard His name spoken by a believer, they must bow the knee and obey.

> "...**that at the name of Jesus every knee should bow, of those in heaven, and of those on earth, and of those under the earth...**" Philippians 2:10

His "preaching", was the announcement of His victory. After three days Jesus was victorious, having completely disarmed the devil (Col 2:15). All the weapons and armour that the devil trusted in was stripped from him. **The power of sin was completely annihilated through the blood of Christ.**

Because Jesus fulfilled and superseded the law, the devil could not accuse people by means of the law. The grounds for any accusation against a person were taken away through Christ bringing forgiveness, acceptance and justification through the work of the cross. The power of death, sickness, and sin was removed from the devil as the pure Christ of Heaven could not be contained in hell (Acts 2:24).

The only legal foothold the devil has for access and control over humans is sin. Sin is his doorway into the human soul. But Jesus slammed the door shut in the devil's face when he removed sin through the cross. Satan no longer has any way to gain access into a person's life if they are in Christ.

The benefits of the cross obviously only apply if we have accepted Christ and believed the Gospel. The Believers

Study Bible says of Colossians 2:15, that the "public display" Jesus made of the devil was a picture drawn from the triumphant Roman general who would strip his foes and lead them as captives behind his chariot in a victory procession through the streets of Rome before the Caesar. The captured foes and all their nobles were often stripped naked and hobbled, shuffling along behind the chariot of the victorious general, so their humiliation was complete.

5

SET FREE FROM POVERTY

"For you know the grace of our Lord Jesus Christ, that though He was rich, yet for your sakes He became poor, that you through His poverty might become rich."
2 Corinthians 8:9

5

SET FREE FROM POVERTY

In 2 Corinthians 8:9, Paul is referring to the fact that Jesus Christ died without one possession to his name, without one stitch of clothing on His body without any money at all so that he could take poverty to the cross and secure its defeat for those who embrace the saviour.

> **"For you know the grace of our Lord Jesus Christ, that though He was rich, yet for your sakes He became poor, that you through His poverty might become rich."** 2 Corinthians 8:9

This Scripture is couched right in the middle of two chapters written to the Corinthians dealing almost exclusively with the subject of money. Many commentators have great difficulty admitting that this passage is actually dealing with money. In fact, I don't think I've yet found one who agrees that Paul is speaking specifically regarding finances. The most common comment is that it is a reference to spiritual riches.

The Thompson Chain Reference Bible is a wonderful resource and study bible, but at this point he too in the margin describes what Paul is referring to as "spiritual riches"; Jamieson, Fausset and Brown comes the closest saying, "...in the heavenly glory which constitutes His riches, and all other things, so far as is really good for us", Matthew Henry interprets it as, "rich in the love of God, rich in the blessings of the new covenant, rich in the hopes of eternal life." The Word Biblical Commentary, claiming a team of respected international scholars who were "a showcase of the best in evangelical critical scholarship for a new generation", states regarding this verse; *"Here, surely wealth and poverty are ciphers, not for material prosperity and penury but for spiritual exchange as the Incarnate Christ became what we are, so we could become what He is."* For that to be consistent, the scripture would have to read, *"Christ...became (spiritually) poor, that you might become (spiritually) rich."*

This then becomes an absurd, almost blasphemous proposition. To say or even intimate that Jesus Christ was a spiritually poor person is ludicrous. Here is a person who raised the dead, healed the sick, displayed complete prowess over demons and the devil, revealed truths regarding God, man and the entire purpose of God that have withstood every kind of test and scrutiny.

This person was not a spiritually poor person. Rather it was because of His spiritual wealth that he was able to go to the cross and bear away the curses that afflict mankind. Even if we limit His poverty to the time He was on the cross, claiming it was our poverty that He took, are we to conclude that the "hope" (Acts 2:26) he entered into was a spiritually poor position!? To maintain any kind of hope, and faith through His ordeal demonstrates an extraordinary spiritual richness. In our effort to read more into the statement than is actually there we make fools of ourselves and prevent God fulfilling His great promises in our lives. Jesus became poor regarding the wealth of this world on the cross, that those who receive Him may become rich with the wealth of this world.

Right at this point many people, (mostly Christians) have a terrible amount of trouble accepting that fact. The scheme of the devil has been to deceive the Church into believing that it is far more pious to be poor than it is to be rich. Suspicion is cast upon those who have accumulated wealth. God is seen as one who would rather his people be poor than enjoy abundance in their world. **Abundance has always been the will of God for His people.**

Getting over a poverty mindset however, is a lot more difficult than most realise. A spirit of religiosity is at the root of this consciousness. Paul encountered it as early as the first century when dealing with the errors of the Colossian church.

> **"Let no one cheat you of your reward, taking delight in false humility and worship of angels, intruding into those things which he has not seen, vainly puffed up by his fleshly mind..."**
> Colossians 2:18

The religious spirit enjoys being ascetic because it draws pride from the effort. This spiritual indulgence actually only severs a person from Christ. As Esau was cheated out of his inheritance so the believer can be cheated out of theirs. Asceticism, (self inflicted austerity and poverty) posing as spirituality cheats believers out of all the blessings Christ has won for them through the work of the cross. The thinking that says high spirituality is at the expense of physical blessing defrauds the believer of their inheritance, whereas the Word causes us to gain it (Act 20:32). Paul is referring to Christianity that poses as Christianity, "humility." This word is taken from Greek words translated *"depressed, that is figuratively speaking, humiliated in circumstances or disposition, not joyful but base, cast down, humble, of low degree and estate."*

We are called to humility, but not servility that embraces poverty and depression as though it were a piety that pleases the Father.

The other word for this "humility" ("tapeinophrosune"), is taken from "phren" meaning to rein in or curb the midriff (as a partition of the body). That is figuratively speaking reigning in the feelings and heart and by extension the mind and understanding (cognitive abilities) as well. This then is saying that smallness (the reigning in) of feelings and mind is promoted by the religious spirit again as if this pleases God, but it actually cheats us out of our inheritance in Christ.

The church has been notorious for thinking small, poor and backward, and then justifying all this because it is "for the Lord." This is saying we do things small and second rate because it's for the Lord. This is ridiculous. God wants us to think bigger than we ever have before. We are not to limit God with our thinking but release Him with ever increasing largeness and release of dreaming of great exploits for Him.

Right from the start those who have pleased God have enjoyed abundance in their lives.

Abraham became exceedingly prosperous as he obeyed God.

> "**Abram was very rich in livestock, in silver, and in gold.**" Genesis 13:2

His son Isaac also prospered as the blessing of abundance promised Abraham also came upon his descendants.

> "**Then Isaac sowed in that land, and reaped in the same year a hundredfold; and the LORD blessed him.**" Genesis 26:12
>
> "**The man began to prosper, and continued prospering until he became very prosperous...**" Genesis 26:13
>
> "**...for he had possessions of flocks and possessions of herds and a great number of servants. So the Philistines envied him.**" Genesis 26:14

These people recognised the blessing of God was upon their lives because God had blessed them. The sons of Isaac were also blessed. As Jacob honoured God in tithing as his grandfather Abraham had, he received a great abundance from the Lord.

> **"Now Jacob ... has acquired all this wealth."**
> Genesis 31:1

Even Job who also lived round the time of Abraham was very wealthy. In fact he was considered to be the wealthiest man in the East.

> **"Also, his possessions were seven thousand sheep, three thousand camels, five hundred yoke of oxen, five hundred female donkeys, and a very large household, so that this man was the greatest of all the people of the East."** Job 1:3

This is the man that God was willing to challenge the devil over. God believed that Job would remain true to the Lord, no matter what happened to him, whether he had nothing, or everything. The devil was granted permission to afflict the man with some of the worst sufferings we could read of, yet Job did remain true to the Lord. His wealth had not corrupted his soul, but rather increased his sensitivity to the needs of those around him.

Moses and Aaron received the tithes of all the priests who had received the tithes of all the people (Num 18:28).

There were 600,000 men in Israel at that time. If we were to give two thirds of them employment at $250 weekly, that's a $25 tithe multiplied by 400,000. That equals $10 million, the tithe of which is $1million. This belonged to Moses and his brother (Num 18:26). That adds up to about $52 million a year! This shows just how small our current day thinking is in this area. You would have to agree that the figures in these equations are conservative in today's world.

Someone might say, "But that was while they were wandering in the wilderness and they all had nothing much anyway. This is ridiculous thinking. They had literally plundered Egypt on the way out, and the laws Moses was instituting were designed for when they entered Canaan. While this was meant to happen shortly after they had departed from Egypt, they were waylaid by their own unbelief at the sight of the giants. God had the largest people on Earth build the mightiest cities, plant the greatest farmlands in some of the best climate on the planet; all for His people Israel. All they had to do was go and take it. The only difficulty they would face was to oust the giants. God would be with them and the whole exercise was to be reasonably easy. However, they stumbled in their faith and wandered for forty years in the wilderness, not experiencing the abundance the Father had already prepared for them. This is much like the church in many areas to day. We have seen giants in the land and been scared off going in and taking what God has prepared for us. This life in Christ is meant to be an abundant one, at every level. We are not saved to become paupers in the Earth. **Jesus died to set us free from poverty.**

King David was also extraordinarily wealthy, so much so that he was able to give $2,835,000,000, ie. $2.8 billion of gold over and above his regular offerings for the building of the temple (1Chron 29:4).

Twenty two times he refers to the offerings he brought into the House of God, his tithing, and the fulfilment of the pledges he had made to God. All this is part of the process by which the Lord brings blessing upon our lives.

King Solomon, the son of King David invited the Queen of Sheba to his palace. She was also extremely wealthy but was breath taken at the expanse of the wealth of Solomon (1Kings 10).

Even the prophets were not considered poor. Isaiah was considered to have come from a wealthy background, Jonah had enough money to purchase a ticket on a boat to a distant country, and Jeremiah was able to go out and buy an acreage for 17 shekels (about $9,000—one shekel equalled 4 days wages) when the Lord told him to (Jer 32:9).

Jesus Himself received gold, frankincense and myrrh at his birth. From early antiquity it was diplomatically correct for kings to bring extravagant gifts to others kings, whether infant or grown, when they visited them for whatever reason.

We have texts from as far back as 1850 BC related to the Ancient Near East, from the city of Mari recording the vast inventories of gifts that were exchanged between kings of greater or lesser degrees when they were meeting each other. They reveal prodigious quantities of gold, ebony, and ivory, lapis lazuli, garments and sweet oil; sent in each direction as part of diplomatic protocol. Even though the amounts of these gifts add up to incredible sums, they pale in ordinariness compared to the first millennium BC practices. Osorkon (889 BC) gave gifts to Egypt totalling 445 metric tons of gold in the form of vessels, statues, furnishings and the like. Gifts came with the Queen of Sheba to the court of Solomon in an extraordinary abundance. However, the record tells us her breath was taken away at the grandeur of Solomon's obvious wealth. There are an abundance of records detailing what was considered diplomatically correct in the amounts of gift giving. In fact if a king's wealth was not represented in his gift, or the stature of the receiving king reflected sufficiently abundantly, the receiving king would let the giver understand in no uncertain terms that he had been slighted by the meanness of the gift.

The number of the Magi was not limited necessarily to just three because there were three categories of gifts mentioned in the Scripture. There were probably many more, and the gifts were not three single items of gold, frankincense and myrrh, but rather, these were the headings of inventories under which many different items would have been included. This was the norm for recording indexes of gifts for kings.

The wealth and influence of the Magi is clearly considerable because of the impact their coming had upon Herod.

This set Jesus up for life. The gifts were for Him, not His family, yet it would be reasonable to suggest that once He understood what his wealth was, He would have shared it with His earthly family.

During His ministry, Jesus was provided for by wealthy women, who followed Him as He travelled.

> **"...and Joanna the wife of Chuza, Herod's steward, and Susanna, and many others who provided for Him from their substance."**
> Luke 8:3

These people were wealthy and there were many of them. They provided all of the Messiah's needs. Jesus' little band received so much, they needed a treasurer; Judas. It was at the Cross "He became poor."

Paul travelled three times around the world, had enough to pay for a Roman trial, and was kept in prison for two years by the Roman procurator of Judea, Felix. The sole reason for his captivity was that he hoped for a bribe from the apostle. He would not have waited that long for a small amount. He knew Paul could deliver and waited for that (Acts 24:26).

Paul tells Philemon to put on his account anything the runaway slave Onesimus owed him. This could have been any amount, yet Paul was confident that he could pay. The Apostle supported an entire ministry team that travelled the world with him. As he laboured at his craft he prospered because of the blessing God had placed on his life. (Acts 20:34).

Paul, who was a strict Pharisee, would have observed tithing as a regular practice all his life. He preached on giving abundantly, and also laying aside at the beginning of each week those first fruits of a persons' prosperity. He fully accepted that Christians would prosper.

> **"On the first day of the week let each one of you lay something aside, storing up as he may prosper..."** 1 Corinthians 16:2

Those people who believe Christians should not prosper ought to become committed to being poor. If we are not meant to prosper, then it would be only logical that God is wanting us to be poor and to fail in life so that we don't succeed and become prosperous. This means He does not want us to do well in life. He does not want us to be blessed with good things, with an abundance for our lives and those of others. If God wants His children to be poor (while He lives in the vast abundances and glories of Heaven), then we should certainly not be living in countries where the government will look after us in our poverty. We should be off to India, where we mark out a piece of the pavement for our home, or live in a cardboard box, and certainly not look for any wealth for medical needs or food. We should scrape around rubbish tins looking for scraps of food along with the rest of the poor. This is what being poor is. If it is the will of God for us to be poor then should we not do it with all our might, become poor like the poorest? By now most say,

"Don't be ridiculous. We're not talking about that kind of poor. We should have enough to just get by moderately."

"How much?"

"Just enough to get by."

"For who to just get by?"

"You!"

That has to be about the most selfish kind of Christianity ever postulated. How are you going to pay your neighbour's rent when they're out of a job? How will you be able to pick up a person who has been run over, robbed, beaten and left half dead on the side of the road? How will you be able to take them to the hospital and then tell them you'll pay whatever it takes to get them healed. Jesus said a true believer is someone who pays the price for the healing of the people who are wounded (Luke 10:33).

This is not talking about spiritual healing either. James says mere religious talk is futile (James 2:16). Real religion is when we physically help people. This is impossible without the means to do it. God wills that we enjoy an abundance in our lives so that we are able to assist others.

> **"...and God is able to make all grace abound toward you, that you, always having all sufficiency in all things, may have an abundance for every good work."** 2 Corinthians 9:8

This is one of the largest and most wonderful Scriptures in the Bible. This says that God will cause an abundance to come into our lives, because of his grace towards us. Even though we don't deserve grace, even though we have done nothing to merit His favour, He has chosen to place this on our lives, and it manifests in abundance.

This is the will of God, that we enjoy an abundance not just on payday, not just when the tax refund comes through, not just when we get a bonus, not just when we receive an inheritance; but always. That means every single day of our lives. God desires that we enjoy a complete sufficiency in all things, so there is not one area we are insufficient in. But there's more! Paul goes on to declare that abundance is decreed for our lives, so we can engage in every good work. We may think we're just going to get involved in giving to one missionary, or supporting a particular ministry, or to give to just one or two people who have needs. Yet the Lord wants us to have such abundance that we can be a blessing to every good work. This is what the church is meant to be. We are meant to have such a prosperity in the church that we are able to give to the needs of those around us all of the time, in abundance.

6

SET FREE FROM THE CURSE OF THE LAW

"If Jesus died to remove the curse, then that is what has happened. The curse has been removed!"

6

SET FREE FROM THE CURSE OF THE LAW

> **"Christ has redeemed us from the curse of the law, having become a curse for us (for it is written, 'Cursed is everyone who hangs on a tree'), that the blessing of Abraham might come upon the Gentiles in Christ Jesus, that we might receive the promise of the Spirit through faith."** Galatians 3:13,14

In fact Paul declares there is not a blessing available that we haven't received.

> **"Blessed be the God and Father of our Lord Jesus Christ, who has blessed us with every spiritual blessing in the heavenly places in Christ..."** Ephesians 1:3

The curse of the law is outlined in Leviticus 26 and Deuteronomy 28, and makes for hair-raising reading. Obedience to the law meant incredible blessing, yet disobedience brought astonishing judgement. The terrible point about the law is that it was impossible to keep (according to Paul), so therefore the curses of these two passages are inevitable for those who do not know the Lord. The curse brought terrible catastrophes upon the circumstances of those affected. The death of Jesus was to disarm the power of these curses.

> "**...but it shall come to pass, if you do not obey the voice of the LORD your God, to observe carefully all His commandments and His statutes which I command you today, that all these curses will come upon you and overtake you... Cursed shall you be in the city, and cursed shall you be in the country.**" Deuteronomy 28:15,16

This meant that life in the city would be cursed. The market place, the entertainment, the justice systems, the education, the hospitals, the religious establishments, the transport and communications, the media, the sporting world, the industries, the finances, the banking systems, the housing; the whole of the circumstances of the city would be cursed. Like wise the countryside, all of the grain crops, the dairy produce, the animal farms, the rivers, the rainfall, the seed for planting, the harvesting, the weather, the health of the crops and the animals, all would come under the curse.

> "**Cursed shall be your basket and your kneading bowl.**" Deuteronomy 28:17

This meant that whatever was taken in the field for preparation in the house would either not be enough, or be of poor quality. The kneading bowl would not bring enough dough for cooking to satisfy the family. The food preparation would be insufficient or else the food would taste terrible and have little nourishment.

Because Christ has sacrificed His life to remove the curse we are blessed with more than enough. All the food is blessed. It tastes great and there is an abundance of it.

> **"Cursed shall be the fruit of your body and the produce of your land, the increase of your cattle and the offspring of your flocks."**
> Deuteronomy 28:18

Your sons and daughters would bring you trouble and difficulty. They would be a curse to you instead of a blessing. That is, if you managed to even have children, because the curse would descend on the womb and render it barren. Even the produce of the land would not reproduce. It would fail to give you seed to sow for next year's crop. Your cattle and sheep would not reproduce. They would be barren, and what they do bring forth would be so inferior it will useless for selling or even using on the farm.

Christ died to remove the curses. Our sons and daughters will be a blessing. Infertile couples will bear children. There will not only be enough but there will be an abundance left over. There will not just be a maintaining of what is already in existence but there will be an unending increase of the blessing upon people's lives, because of the work of the Cross.

> **"Cursed shall you be when you come in, and cursed shall you be when you go out."**
> Deuteronomy 28:19

Under the curse when you came into the house, things would go wrong and homecoming would not be pleasant. Your house would not be a refuge. It would be a place you want to get away from. Even when you went out things would go wrong. The car would break down. Accidents would happen. You may have planned to have a good time, but it would be miserable, because it would not go as you hoped. It would all just be miserable. You would receive fines for parking in the wrong spot, or for speeding. People would steal things from you and you would wish you hadn't gone out.

When we receive Christ, the good news is that the curse is removed. Coming home is beautiful. Your home is a refuge. Your car works well. When you go out, you have a good time. Protection covers your home, and your belongings. Even if things do go wrong they will be forced to turn around for good because there is no curse on you, instead you carry the blessing of God.

> **"The LORD will send on you cursing, confusion, and rebuke in all that you set your hand to do, until you are destroyed and until you perish quickly, because of the wickedness of your doings in which you have forsaken Me."**
> Deuteronomy 28:20

Under the curse you would be confused and not know what to do. You would seek guidance and get none. You would try to make decisions but never feel confident about anything. You would attempt to start a business and although you might have had all the statistics saying it would go well, it would not because of the curse and rebuke from God upon all that you set your hand to. Because the curse has been removed because of Christ's death, all confusion is also removed. You are set free to make clear-minded decisions. Even a little effort is rewarded in a big way. Because the blessing rests on you, you make strong decisions that work well for you.

> "**The LORD will make the plague cling to you until He has consumed you from the land which you are going to possess.**" Deuteronomy 28:21

> "**The LORD will strike you with consumption, with fever, with inflammation, with severe burning fever, with the sword, with scorching, and with mildew; they shall pursue you until you perish.**" Deuteronomy 28:22

Under the curse physical sicknesses would cling to you, and would not go away. It would literally cling to you even though you take all kinds of medication to make it go away. Some of the sicknesses that would cling include "consumption", (which has been identified as pulmonary tuberculosis–phthisis or as the side effects of wasting and emaciation from prolonged bouts of malarial fever—some have even suggested cancer); "fever", (refers to any number of diseases: malaria, typhoid, typhus, dysentery, chronic diarrhoea, or cholera); "inflammation", when injury becomes worse rather than better and the healing processes of the body fail, or become infected; "the sword", refers to being struck by the sword and wounded by the effects of war; "scorching and mildew", refers to drought and diseases that would come upon the crops of Israel so that they would fail to come to fruit. All these would follow after the Israelites because of the curse of the law, "until they would perish."

Christ absorbed the curse in His body and then annihilated through His death, all the terrible plagues identified. Neither sickness, nor war, nor plagues upon people and crops, will not fail on you. Others may get sick with these diseases but you will avoid them. These illnesses will not rest on you because you are under the blessing, not the curse.

> **"And your heavens which are over your head shall be bronze, and the earth which is under you shall be iron. The LORD will change the rain of your land to powder and dust; from the heaven it shall come down on you until you are destroyed."** Deuteronomy 28:23,24

Under the curse, drought would ravage the land so that the earth become as hard as iron and dust would cover the sky rather than rain; "until destruction comes." When a nation embraces Christ as it's Saviour, the curse is broken and the blessing of God overtakes all the curses, breaking the worst of conditions, in this case, for an agricultural community, drought.

> **"The LORD will cause you to be defeated before your enemies; you shall go out one way against them and flee seven ways before them; and you shall become troublesome to all the**

> **kingdoms of the earth. Your carcasses shall be food for all the birds of the air and the beasts of the earth, and no one shall frighten them away."**
> Deuteronomy 28v25,26

Under the curse instead of defeating your enemies they would defeat you. Notice the Word says you will have enemies, yet under the curse they would defeat you, but under the blessing you would triumph over them. Under the curse you would flee from the opposition. You would not be favoured by the nations, but rather be a nuisance to the nations of the Earth. The people of the Earth would be happy to see you destroyed by the birds and beasts. Under the blessing it is important for the church to accept that it is the light of this world, the church holds the answer. Instead, often the church has been considered a nuisance and perceived to have no value.

> **"The LORD will strike you with the boils of Egypt, with tumours, with the scab, and with the itch, from which you cannot be healed. The LORD will strike you with madness and blindness and confusion of heart."**
> Deuteronomy 28:27

Under the curse the sicknesses of the world would come upon you; the boils—a general Bible term to describe inflamed swellings of the skin; (the Hebrew word literally means ulcers); tumours—a disease most commentators find difficult to identify yet agree is regarded as fatal; the scab and the itch—which refers to skin diseases such as eczema, leprosy, scales and ringworm. Incurable diseases were predicted to be part of the curse. Insanity, blindness and confusion would also come upon those that were under the curse of the law.

With the curse removed, the sicknesses of the world have no access into our lives. Through the blessing of God we will be struck with good health, and healing of any illness that may occur. We will be stricken with sanity, vision and peace in our hearts.

> "**...and you shall grope at noonday, as a blind man gropes in darkness; you shall not prosper in your ways; you shall be only oppressed and plundered continually, and no one shall save you.**" Deuteronomy 28:29

Under the curse oppressors and those who wished to take advantage of you would overcome you. You would be "ripped off" again and again and wonder why. **The curse of the law rests upon the person who has not received Christ.** Generally there is at least someone who will seek to help the unfortunate out of their plight, but not so under these conditions. No one will come to your aid. As this curse and all others is removed, we will be released from things that bind us, set free from oppressors and instead of being taken advantage of, we will be blessed with great business deals, enormous bargains, incredible bonuses. If we do find ourselves in difficulty, people will come to our aid and help us to find a way out of the problem.

> **"You shall betroth a wife, but another man shall lie with her; you shall build a house, but you shall not dwell in it; you shall plant a vineyard, but shall not gather its grapes.**

> **Your ox shall be slaughtered before your eyes, but you shall not eat of it; your donkey shall be violently taken away from before you, and shall not be restored you; your sheep shall be given to your enemies, and you shall have no one to rescue them. Your sons and your daughters shall be given to another people, and your eyes shall look and fail with longing for them all day long; and there shall be no strength in your hand. A nation whom you have not known shall eat the fruit of your land and the produce of your labour, and you shall be only oppressed and crushed continually. So you shall be driven mad because of the sight which your eyes see."**
> Deuteronomy 28:30-34

Under the curse all sense of security would depart from you. Another person would sleep with your wife. You would build your own home, but not live in it. For one reason or another, someone else would live in the house you thought you were building for yourself. You would start a business but someone else would buy it out and reap all the benefits of it. This is the curse of the law. You work hard at obtaining and creating something but others reap the benefits. All your inventions, hard work and efforts would reap nothing because others would take away your employees, your management team, your workers and your clients—all would be taken from you. Your children would depart from you and your heart will break over longing for them to be with you yet you would not have any ability to win them back. Strangers, not even family or friends would eat and enjoy all the hard work you've put in. All these conditions would produce instability of mind, as a kind of madness sets in. Through the blessing of God, free from the curse because of the death of Jesus Christ, your spouse will remain faithful, the home and business you build will be blessed and you and your family will eat the fruit of your labour. Clients, employees, family members, will be loyal to you. You will enjoy great peace of mind as you and your family and friends enjoy the blessing of Heaven.

> **"The LORD will strike you in the knees and on the legs with severe boils which cannot be healed, and from the sole of your foot to the top of your head."** Deuteronomy 28:35

These sound like the kind of boils Job had (Job 2:7), which have been identified with smallpox or with treponematosis (a parasitic infection).

> **"The LORD will bring you and the king whom you set over you to a nation which neither you nor your fathers have known, and there you shall serve other gods; wood and stone."** Deuteronomy 28:36

The worst thing about these curses is that the glory of God would no longer be among you, but rather the lifeless gods of mere wood and stone, which give no glory at all to those who serve them. You would be transported out of the kingdom of God into a strange land, where you would have no friends, but only strangers.

Maybe the greatest blessing we can know, set free from the curse, is the presence of God in our lives, at home, at work, in the car, on holiday, in family life, in solitary life. God is with us. This is the greatest blessing of the New Testament. This is the reason that Jesus suffered such a torturous death to connect us with His Father and to remain in fellowship with Him.

> "**...and you shall become an astonishment, a proverb, and a byword among all nations where the LORD will drive you.**" Deuteronomy 28:37

Under the curse respect is lost and mockery is inherited. The inhabitants of the lands to which you would be sent would hate you. People would make fun of you, and joke about you. Under the blessing of God, the people of God find respect and are often feared. Godly people become the most prosperous and exercise influential leadership through natural and supernatural means. Their words come to pass and they express practical compassion that ensures they are valued above all others in the community. The action of servanthood makes them indispensable and accompanying acts of God guarantee they are reverenced.

> "**You shall carry much seed out to the field but gather little in, for the locust shall consume it. You shall plant vineyards and tend them, but you shall neither drink of the wine nor gather the grapes; for the worms shall eat them. You shall have olive trees throughout all your territory, but you shall not anoint yourself with the oil; for your olives shall drop off. You shall beget sons and daughters, but they shall not be yours; for they shall go into captivity. Locusts shall consume all your trees and the produce of your land.**" Deuteronomy 28:38-42

Under the curse all your efforts to produce crops, build businesses, plant orchards, raise stock would fail because of diseases, and insects that would destroy them. Even your sons and daughters would be of no value to you, but rather a grief because strangers would steal them away into slavery and captivity.

Freedom from the curse guarantees your seed will produce the maximum possible, your harvest will come in, your business will grow. Your stock will increase. Your sons and daughters will be of benefit to you, not just a burden. You will not be weighed down with debt reducing your capacity to enjoy life. The blessing upon you will accelerate your earning ability, increase your business, and bless the results.

> **"The alien who is among you shall rise higher and higher above you, and you shall come down lower and lower. He shall lend to you, but you shall not lend to him; he shall be the head, and you shall be the tail."** Deuteronomy 28:43,44

Under the curse those who are strangers and foreigners amongst you in your own land and your own houses would rise up to rule over you in civic government areas, financial areas, business, entertainment, sports and education, so that you are servile to them. They would lend money to you and you would be "wagged" like the tail, whilst they were the head.

Because you receive Christ and His work on the cross is effective in obliterating the curse of the law, you will rise, in humility, higher and higher. The power of "lift" will be in you. Instead of you seeking money from the world, the world will be seeking money from you. You will gain the control and the power of direction as in being the head and not the tail. The blessing of God brings the power of influence, so that the people of God change society. This comes because they gain power through financial abundance, or through elevation to positions of power. Under the curse we lose the ability to effect but under the blessing effectiveness becomes a gift from God.

> "**Moreover all these curses shall come upon you and pursue and overtake you, until you are destroyed, because you did not obey the voice of the LORD your God, to keep His commandments and His statutes which He commanded you...and they shall be upon you for a sign and a wonder, and on your descendants forever. Because you did not serve the LORD your God with joy and gladness of heart, for the abundance of everything...therefore you shall serve your enemies, whom the LORD will send against you, in hunger, in thirst, in nakedness, and in need of everything; and He will put a yoke of iron on your neck until He has destroyed you.**" Deuteronomy 28:45-48

Because of your disobedience to the Lord, these curses would eventually overwhelm and destroy you, until you were in slavery to foreigners and in abject poverty: in need of everything.

Under the blessing of God the curses are continually lifted off us until none are left. We serve the Lord with joy and gladness of heart, and instead of hunger and thirst and nakedness, we are filled with good food and drink and dressed in the best. We are in need of nothing.

> "The LORD will bring a nation against you from afar, from the end of the earth, as swift as the eagle flies, a nation whose language you will not understand...a nation of fierce countenance, which does not respect the elderly nor show favour to the young. ...and they shall eat the increase of your livestock and the produce of your land, until you are destroyed; they shall not leave you grain or new wine or oil, or the increase of your cattle or the offspring of your flocks, until they have destroyed you.
>
> They shall besiege you at all your gates until your high and fortified walls, in which you trust, come down throughout all your land; and they shall besiege you at all your gates throughout all your land which the LORD your God has given you. You shall eat the fruit of your own body, the flesh of your sons and your daughters whom the LORD your God has given you, in the siege and desperate straits in which your enemy shall distress you.
>
> The sensitive and very refined man among you will be hostile toward his brother, toward the wife of his bosom, and toward the rest of his children whom he leaves behind...so that he will not give any of them the flesh of his children whom he will eat, because he has nothing left in the siege and desperate straits in which

> **your enemy shall distress you at all your gates.**
>
> **The tender and delicate woman among you, who would not venture to set the sole of her foot on the ground because of her delicateness and sensitivity, will refuse to the husband of her bosom, and to her son and her daughter...her placenta which comes out from between her feet and her children whom she bears; for she will eat them secretly for lack of everything in the siege and desperate straits in which your enemy shall distress you at all your gates."**
> Deuteronomy 28:49-57

Because of the curse, merciless and fierce enemies would come against you who would completely destroy you and besiege you to the point where you would be debased to do terrible things even to your own family such as destroying your own children.

Under the blessing you cannot be overwhelmed by enemies. Should an enemy attack they will not win. Your cities, houses and families will be secure. Instead your children grow up, developed to their full potential, blessed in every way.

> **"If you do not carefully observe all the words of this law that are written in this book, that you may fear this glorious and awesome name, THE LORD YOUR GOD...then the LORD will bring upon you and your descendants extraordinary plagues; great and prolonged plagues; and serious and prolonged sicknesses."**
> Deuteronomy 28:58,59

Plagues that have never even been heard of would come upon those who have this curse upon them. They would last for extraordinarily long times, be unusually large, and be of such an unusual nature there would be no cure for them.

Under the blessing of God, you will be set free from plagues that are attacking everyone else. If you do get sick, it will not last long. You will get over illness quickly.

> **"Moreover He will bring back on you all the diseases of Egypt, of which you were afraid, and they shall cling to you. Also every sickness and every plague, which is not written in this Book of the Law, will the LORD bring upon you until you are destroyed. You shall be left few in number, whereas you were as the stars of heaven in multitude, because you would not obey the voice of the LORD your God."** Deuteronomy 28:60-62

Under the curse you would become pathetically few in number rather than a vast multitude and therefore your power, nobility, and strength amongst others would become nothing.

Because we are set free from the curse, the church will increase more and more throughout the Earth. Under the blessing we will outstrip the numbers of people who are not saved, in the world.

> **"...and it shall be, that just as the LORD rejoiced over you to do you good and multiply you, so the LORD will rejoice over you to**

> **destroy you and bring you to nothing; and you shall be plucked from off the land which you go to possess."** Deuteronomy 28:63

Under the curse God Himself would be happy to destroy you because you were such an offence and grief to Him. He would cause you to be removed from your homeland where all your fond memories, family relationships, and possessions were. You would be sent to a land where you have no history or sense of belonging.

Set free from the curse, God's only joy is to see you happy, blessed and living in victory. His great joy is to multiply you and do you good. His determination is that you dwell safely in the land.

> **"Then the LORD will scatter you among all peoples, from one end of the earth to the other, and there you shall serve other gods, which neither you nor your fathers have known; wood and stone...and among those nations you shall find no rest, nor shall the sole of your foot have a resting place; but there the LORD will give you a trembling heart, failing eyes, and anguish of soul. Your life shall hang in doubt before you; you shall fear day and night, and have no assurance of life. In the morning you shall say, "Oh, that it were evening!" And at evening you shall say, "Oh, that it were morning!" because of the fear which terrifies your heart, and because of the sight which your eyes see."** Deuteronomy 28:64-67

Under the curse you would experience restlessness, anxiety and never enjoy security, stability or peacefulness. Your heart would be anxious and panic stricken as you were without vision for the future. Your soul would be in pain and anguish. You would be doubtful about whether or not you are going to live and yet you would never feel safe about your well-being. You would wish that your life was over and that your days would be over quickly so that you no longer experience the terror and fear of your life.

Free from the curse, you are secure, safe, restful not restless. Your life will not be in doubt, but you will be completely assured of the blessing. Instead of fear filling your heart, faith will overwhelm all your doubts. The vision you have of the future will cause you to be inspired and enthused with fresh energy.

> **"...and the LORD will take you back to Egypt in ships, by the way of which I said to you, "You shall never see it again." And there you shall be offered for sale to your enemies as male and female slaves, but no one will buy you."**
> Deuteronomy 28:68

Under the curse you would be taken back to places you never wanted to return to. Your whole life would seem to go backwards, and there you would try to at least eke out a living but no one would want you or employ you. The final and most terrible thing would be that you were rejected and not wanted by anybody.

Under the blessing of God you progress. You move forward. You will be the one calling the shots.

If Jesus has died to remove the curse then that is what has happened, the curse has been removed. For a curse to be effective it must have grounds for resting on someone's life. Once the blood of Christ has washed all sins from our soul, there remains no more ground for any curse whatsoever to gain access to our world.

> **"Like a flitting sparrow, like a flying swallow, so a curse without cause shall not alight."**
> Proverbs 26:2

This means that all those curses have been removed and reversed, so that under the blessing of God, instead of curses, blessings shower down on our lives in all the areas that were cursed under the law.

It means our life in the city is blessed. The market place, the entertainment, the justice systems, the world of education, hospitals, the religious establishments, transport and communications, the media, the sporting world, industries, the banking systems, the housing; the whole of the circumstances of the city will be blessed. Like wise the countryside, all of the grain crops, the dairy produce, the animal farms, the rivers, the rainfall, the seed for planting, the harvesting, the weather, the health of the crops and the animals, all would come under the blessing of God.

Whatever is taken in the field, for preparation in the house, will be more than enough, and the very best quality. The food preparation will be abundant and taste fantastic with super-nourishment.

Your sons and daughters will bring ease and blessing. They

will be a blessing to you instead of a curse. You will have beautiful children and not be barren, because the blessing will rest on the womb and render it fruitful. Even the produce of the land will multiply with abundance. Seed is in full supply to sow for next year's crop. Your cattle and sheep will reproduce. They will not be barren, and what they do bring forth would be superior to anything else your competition can produce.

When you come into the house, things will go well and homecoming will be a joyful occasion. Your house will be a refuge. It will be your castle to retreat to from the pressure of the world. When you step out of your home things would work well for you. The car will run well. Accidents will be avoided. If there is a breakdown or an accident it will work together for good. Your plans will come to fruition. You will not be besieged by troubles, and your goods will be safe from thieves.

You know exactly what to do. You will seek guidance and become clear about your direction. You will make decisions and feel confident about them. You will start a business and it will go well because of the blessing from God upon all that you set your hand to.

Physical health will rest upon you. Any sicknesses or wounds that you do incur will heal swiftly. Any medical procedures will be completely successful.

Rain will drench the land so that the earth becomes soft.

Instead of being defeated by your enemies you will defeat them. Notice the Word says you will have enemies, yet under the curse the enemy would defeat you, but under the blessing you would triumph over them. Under the blessing your enemies will flee from you. You will be favoured by the nations. The people of the Earth will be happy to see you blessed.

Incurable disease will disappear from you. Healing will come from God.

You will overcome oppressors and those who wished to take advantage of you. When you are in trouble people will come to your aid and give you help.

Great security is upon you with the blessing of God. Your marriage is secure. You will enjoy living in the home you build. You will reap the benefits of the business you build. Under the blessing of God, in fact you will reap where others have laboured. You will benefit from those who thought to harm you. You children will inherit your wealth. You will see your children grow in God and good health. You will bless others, friends, families and strangers. You will enjoy a great peace of mind and sanity that comes from a secure life free from anxiety.

The glory of God will manifest among you. You will worship and delight in God. You will be planted in the kingdom of God with many friends, good support, leaders and a future.

People will come to you for guidance and coaching. They will look to you for leadership. They will use you as an example for living.

Strangers will not rule over you but rather you will be able to guide and bless them because of the blessing of God upon you.

You multiply in number becoming a vast multitude and your power, nobility, and strength amongst others will increase.

God Himself will be happy to bless you because you were such a blessing to Him. He will cause you to be established in your homeland where all your fond memories, family relationships, and possessions are.

You would experience rest, security, stability and peacefulness. Your heart would be calm and full of faith with vision for the future. Your soul would be in joy and health. You would be full of faith about your future.

You will be taken to places you always wanted to go. Your whole life will move forward. People everywhere will seek you out to be your friend, to be connected to you. This is just the beginning of the great blessing of God.

7

SET FREE FROM SELF

"For the law of the Spirit of life in Christ Jesus has made me free from the law of sin and death."
Romans 8:2

7

SET FREE FROM SELF

We must realise that Jesus did not live, die, or even rise from the dead for Himself. He did it all for us. His perfect life is imputed to us for righteousness (Jer 23:6). We are counted as righteous as Jesus was, because His life has been freely imputed to our account.

This is one of the most awesome facts of our salvation. Jesus lived a perfect life. Scripture describes His life as "without spot or blemish" (1 Pet 1:19). He was perfect in His relationship with God. He was perfect in His relationships with other people, His family, community, and friends. He was perfect in His moral life. Perfect in thought. Perfect in attitude. Perfect in motivation. Perfect in speech. Perfect in action. Perfect in obedience and calling. Perfect in pleasing the Father. Jesus was sinless. Without sin. Without fault. Perfect! Jeremiah says in his writings (Jer 23:6), there will come a day when the Lord will be known as Jehovah-Tsidkenu, literally meaning, "the Lord our righteousness." This is the kernel of our justification before God. We are declared righteous, perfect, not because we are, but because Jesus is. The Lord Himself is our righteousness. Let me explain a little further.

After the resurrection Jesus appears before the Father. He presents His life. The Father views this life. He declares it perfect. In fact, it is the life God would live if He had became a human. And that is exactly the case. Jesus, being our advocate, explains to the Father that Phil Pringle down on planet Earth desires to be right with God, to enter Heaven and have a relationship with God. The Father replies that it's out of the question; hopeless. He fully knows the life of Phil Pringle. It falls far too short of the glory of God. It is full of faults and shortcomings, sins and iniquities. But Jesus says to the Father that He wants to "give" His perfect life to the man, so he can be saved, acquitted from all guilt, and declared righteous before God in Heaven. The Father agrees that this is a wonderful idea, and accepts the act as legitimate. God is not looking for ways to reject, condemn and curse man. He has always been looking for ways to save him.

This is the perfect way. It is a perfect salvation. The saved person places His trust in the righteousness of Christ, not their own. In terms of righteousness this places us in exactly the same standing before God as Jesus Himself. It places us in the position of being fully qualified to receive all the blessings that are promised throughout Scripture to the righteous. This is "imputed" righteousness. This is salvation. It is the awesome gift of God. It is Jesus Himself being given to our lives. We live by the righteousness of another: the righteousness of Jesus Christ the Perfect. His life has been credited to our account.

His death has removed all sin from our lives, and His resurrection has given us eternal life. He did it all for us, out of love for us. His motive for doing all that He did was love.

One of the most challenging obstacles we have to overcome in this life is ourselves. We are born with a nature that desires to sin. Our flesh has inherent impulses towards wrongdoing. We live in this fleshly nature until we are born again when we have the option to become released from our self-nature and embrace the nature of Christ.

Paul reveals that this nature has been put to death in Christ.

> "**...knowing this, that our old man was crucified with Him, that the body of sin might be done away with, that we should no longer be slaves of sin.**" Romans 6:6

This nature is referred to in the Scripture as the "the old man", "the body of sin", "the old nature", "the flesh." The impulses of this nature are referred to in various Scriptures.

> "**...but now you yourselves are to put off all these: anger, wrath, malice, blasphemy, filthy language out of your mouth. Do not lie to one another, since you have put off the old man with his deeds...**" Colossians 3:8,9

> **"Now the works of the flesh are evident, which are: adultery, fornication, uncleanness, lewdness...idolatry, sorcery, hatred, contentions, jealousies, outbursts of wrath, selfish ambitions, dissensions, heresies...envy, murders, drunkenness, revelries, and the like..."** Galatians 5:19-21

The flesh is born with these inclinations in it. We teach children how to be good. It seems they need little instruction in the art of doing wrong. When we come to Christ, He doesn't offer us a new set of rules to live by. He offers a new spirit. This new life within us overwhelms the power of the flesh. The law of the Holy Spirit is a higher and more powerful law than the law of sin. Both are laws, but one is more powerful than the other. This is like the law of aerodynamics. The law of gravity forces everything down to the Earth, yet another law, the law of aerodynamics, actually overcomes the downward pull and carries us up into the sky.

> **"For the law of the Spirit of life in Christ Jesus has made me free from the law of sin and death."** Romans 8:2

Ezekiel predicted this would happen.

> **"I will give you a new heart and put a new spirit within you; I will take the heart of stone out of your flesh and give you a heart of flesh. I will put My Spirit within you and cause you to walk in My statutes, and you will keep My judgments and do them."** Ezekiel 36:26,27

Without this inward revolution, where the sin nature dies and the nature of righteousness is born, we are engaged in a continual internal war, struggling with the powerful negative woven into the self-nature.

Not only does God deal a deathblow to the sin impulse within, but also to our love for sin. He gives us a new heart. A heart for God. A desire for righteousness. This is an amazing thing. One day we're in love with darkness; the next day we shun it with disgust. We suddenly love the light. One day we're blaspheming the name of Jesus; the next day it's the dearest name under the sun to us. One day we're cursing; the next day we're praying. It happens in a moment. We are born again. A new nature is deposited into our frame.

Paul urges us to live in that zone where we take the initiative and "put on" the new nature whilst "putting off" the old (Eph 4:22-24). We appropriate this reality by feeding the new nature and starving the old. As we live in the Spirit, for the Lord, the old nature is put to death.

> **"For if you live according to the flesh you will die; but if by the Spirit you put to death the deeds of the body, you will live."** Romans 8:13

I've heard it said that one of the punishments for a murderer in ancient Roman times was that the carcass of the victim was chained to the back of the murderer. Eventually the diseases from the decaying corpse ate through into the healthy body of the criminal until he too, died; albeit a slow, horrible death.

This is a very clear picture of what happens to the believer who fails to actually put off the "old nature." It will eventually eat through into the new nature and bring death with it.

The death of the old nature is a combination effort from both the Christian and God. The starting point however, is that Jesus has killed the self-nature in all of us through the cross. The old Adamic nature is killed through the cross. A "new species of being", is created. Jesus is the new Adam of a new race of people, void of the sinful streak that runs so deeply in Adam's line. The trigger that releases this great work of the cross is water baptism.

"Baptism" literally means to "immerse into". The Christian is commanded to be baptised. We are "immersed into";

1. **water** (Acts 2:38,41)

2. **the Holy Spirit** (Mat 3:11)

3. **the Church** (1 Cor 12:13)

4. **fire** (Mat 3:11)

We are immersed, not sprinkled. This is important to grasp, because our death to the old is total, not partial, and our coming alive to the new is also total, not partial.

> **"Or do you not know that as many of us as were baptised into Christ Jesus were baptised into His death? Therefore we were buried with Him through baptism into death, that just as Christ was raised from the dead by the glory of the**

> **Father, even so we also should walk in newness of life. For if we have been united together in the likeness of His death, certainly we also shall be in the likeness of His resurrection…knowing this, that our old man was crucified with Him, that the body of sin might be done away with, that we should no longer be slaves of sin."**
> Romans 6:3-6

The Christian life demands a 100% commitment. It is impossible to live it any other way. Hence we are baptised into those elements that enable us to live this most magnificent of lives. It is interesting to cover a little history here that underscores the importance of total immersion.

The word baptism is an anglicised word. This means that when it was translated into the English language from the Greek it was basically left as it was. There were reasons surrounding this. The translators of the Bible were commissioned to do so by the then King of England, James I. The King of England was also the recognised head of the Church. This responsibility carried over from the days when the Church of England broke away from the Church of Rome. When the Pope refused to grant King Henry VIII a divorce, Henry decided that he would nationalise the church in his country. Thus began the Church of England, the Anglican Church.

In the early church, people were baptised by full immersion. However, as time passed, and for one reason or another, the practice of plunging new believers beneath the water passed away. Carrying out the ceremony only when the believer was of an age to understand the significance of what he was doing also passed away. Babies were baptised as a matter of religious practice, if the parents were members of the Church. Neither did a person's spiritual state seem to matter. The ceremony was enough.

In fact, the ceremony was seen as the process where-by the person became acceptable to God. Thus a person was thought to become a Christian by virtue of his infant baptism. This has always been the danger of religious "acts." Too easily do they degenerate into heartless, empty, lip serving traditions. These are at best false securities. At worst they are vigorous enemies of God and His work in people's hearts.

So the practice of baptism became a ceremony of sprinkling with water for admission to the church. Derek Prince tells us that *"the relationship between James I and his bishops was not always too cordial and he did not wish the new translation of the Bible, published in his name and with his authority, to make his relationship with the bishops any worse. For this reason he allowed it to be understood that as far as possible, nothing was to be introduced into the translation which would cause unnecessary offence to the bishops or which would be too obviously contrary to the practices of the established church. Hence the Greek word 'baptizo' which could easily have become, in translation, a source of controversy, was never translated at all, but was simply written over in the English language."*

The word "bapto" in Greek means "to whelm, to cover wholly with a fluid." It relates to washings and ablutions of all kinds. It is important we understand the full meaning of this word because it relates to areas other than just water baptism such as the baptism in the Holy Spirit, the baptism into Christ's Body, and the baptism of suffering. None of these are a sprinkling experience. They all refer to a complete immersion. If we allow ourselves to think that baptism is ceremonial, participated in without any intelligent understanding of the event, and simply a sprinkling, we will dilute God's work in people's lives to an almost non-existent level. Sadly, this is exactly the case in many Christian expressions.

In 1608 John Smyth baptised himself in Amsterdam. This was basically the beginning of the Baptist movement, as we know it today. This group recovered the vital truth of adult, full immersion as a fulfilment of Christ's command to "be baptised."

Baptism as practised by Christians in the New Testament has its roots in the Old. Noahs flood is a symbol of water baptism. The old generation perished in the water and the new generation was saved. Thus began a whole new world.

> **"the divine longsuffering waited in the days of Noah, while the ark was being prepared, in which a few, that is, eight souls were saved through water. There is also an anti-type that now saves us—baptism..."** 1 Peter 3:20,21

Another baptism picture showing deliverance from the old as we enter the new is Moses crossing the Red Sea with three million Hebrews behind him.

> **"All our fathers were under the cloud and all passed through the sea, all were baptised into Moses in the cloud and in the sea."**
> 1 Corinthians 10:1,2

These are two images taken from events in the Old Testament. However, as a practice, baptism has its beginnings in the Tabernacle of Moses.

The priests were required to cleanse themselves regularly in a large bowl called the "laver." It was positioned immediately after the great bronze altar used for burnt sacrifices to God. The laver itself was made from the donated bronze mirrors of the Israelite women. Parts of the sacrificed animals were also washed in the laver. Thus the concept of cleansing by water as part of our approach to God was firmly in place.

The next historical event predating New Testament baptism is found in 2 Kings 5. It is the story of an Assyrian Commander, Naaman. Although a famous warrior with a powerful position in his nation, he was a leper. One of the foreign maids he had abducted from Israel advised him that there was help to be found in her country. She knew that the prophet Elisha could heal him. The commander became convinced and made the journey to the prophet. Elisha instructed the man to dip himself seven times in the River Jordan to be healed. Although the proud General initially resisted the command, he eventually carried it out. The result; he was completely healed of leprosy. Leprosy is always seen as a symbol of sin in the Old Testament. This obviously sets the stage for John the Baptist at the River Jordan.

He is found in the desert preaching a message of repentance to the Israelites. Those responding to his call must make a public profession that they are in fact leaving sin and turning to righteousness. The sign of their intent is that they are baptised, fully immersed as adults in the River Jordan. It is an outward expression of an internal change of heart.

The Bible tells us that the "whole region" goes out to John. He is experiencing a vast move of God. He knows his purpose, though. It is to prepare the way for another, Jesus. His cousin, Jesus, arrives in the midst of this revival and asks John to baptise Him too. Even though Christ had no sin, he declared that it is necessary to do this in order to "fulfil all righteousness."

After Christ rises from the dead and the Holy Spirit falls, baptism loses none of its significance. It continues as the recognised practice by which people publicly declare their commitment to repent and turn to God. Believers are quickly baptised after conversion.

> "**Then those who gladly received his word were baptised.**" Acts 2:41

Not only does water baptism continue as an accepted practice of the church, but it escalates in importance to being an accompanying act of salvation.

> "**He who believes and is baptised will be saved; but he who does not believe will be condemned.**" Mark 16:16

Baptism gains even further significance for the walk of the believer until Paul arrives on the scene. He proclaims his revelation of the victory we gain through water baptism. As we have said earlier, when we are saved, not only are our sins forgiven but the person who commits those offences, the sinner, is also blotted out. Simply plucking the fruit from a tree, no matter how sour it is, doesn't prevent the tree from continuing to yield the same sour fruit. The tree itself must be killed. However, to "do away" with every believer after they decide for Christ is obviously unacceptable. Yet it is definitely God's will to accomplish this. The bias towards sin is in us the day we are conceived.

> **"Behold, I was brought forth in iniquity and in sin did my mother conceive me."** Psalm 51:5

Baptism in water is our life statement, not only that we turn from sin, but that we are also dying. We are declaring that the entire sum of our old life and the entire sum of our sin nature is dead.

We are also saying that we are being resurrected into a totally new life in Christ. Being lowered into the waters of baptism is being crucified and buried with Christ. Being lifted up out of the water is being resurrected with Christ. Baptism is God's means of identifying us with the death ,burial and resurrection of Jesus Christ. Let's read that awesome Scripture again, awakening us to the fact that our old life has been literally crucified with Christ and that we are now a new creation in Christ.

> **"Or do you not know that as many of us as were baptised into Christ Jesus were baptised into his death? Therefore we were buried with Him through baptism into death, that just as Christ was raised from the dead by the glory of the Father, even so we should walk in newness of life. For if we have been united together in the likeness of his death, certainly we shall also be in the likeness of His resurrection."** Romans 6:3

God is involved in the appropriating of this truth in a major way. The Christian life is not to be something we struggle and strive to be. It is to be as natural as breathing. If we are continually trying to be Christian, this truth needs to come alive in us. Being a Christian is not something I have to think about if I have been born again. I don't struggle to breathe, to digest food: to be a human being. I am created for these things. This is exactly the same as being a Christian. We are created Christian when we come to Christ. "Being" comes before "doing." I'm a human being, before I'm a human doing.

As God takes us through various experiences, some will be painful. It is in these times when the Lord can break us to His will so that we die to ourselves. Deep within us there is a great shaft called "I". Upon this shaft are all the levers of our life. This "I" shaft is the motivator of all we do. When it turns, so do we. All the levers move when "I" moves. What "I" wants to do, I do. However, there comes a day when God takes all our self-centeredness and self will and brings it to death. He breaks it. Though painful, this is one of the greatest days of victory we can ever enjoy. We die. We rest in peace. This is the ultimate repentance; not just when sin dies, but when the sinner dies. God removes that "I" shaft, and replaces it with "Christ." Now He, Jesus, is the deep motivator of our lives, of our actions and attitudes. We can say with Paul,

> **"I have been crucified with Christ; it is no longer I who live, but Christ lives in me..."**
> Galatians 2:20

We are set free from ourselves through the great work of the cross.

8

SET FREE FROM THE WORLD

"...but God forbid that I should boast except in the cross of our Lord Jesus Christ, by whom the world has been crucified to me, and I to the world."
Galatians 6:14

8

SET FREE FROM THE WORLD

Paul declares that because of the cross the world is now dead to me and I am dead to the world. I am no longer under the domination of whatever is happening in this world. I have been transferred to the Kingdom of God. In fact Paul calls it a "translation";

> **"Who hath delivered us from the power of darkness, and hath *translated* us into the kingdom of his dear Son..."**
> Colossians 1:13 *(my emphasis)*

Enoch was "translated" so that he didn't even experience death (Heb 11:5). The Bible says he could not be found because God had "taken" him. We read that Philip the evangelist was "caught away", in much the same way (Acts 8:39) from the Gaza strip road to a town called Azotus. He disappeared from the Ethiopian whom he had just baptised and then immediately appeared at a town about 30 kilometres away. This was a supernatural "translation." We too have been supernaturally "caught away" from one place to land in another. We have been translated from the kingdom of darkness to the kingdom of light. We are no longer under the dominion of the darkness of this world but rather we are now dominated by light.

The word "power" is the Greek word *"exousia"*, meaning "privilege", "authority", ie. force, capacity, competency, freedom, or mastery, magistrate, superhuman, potentate, token of control, delegated influence, jurisdiction, liberty, power, right and/or strength. Whatever is controlling the world no longer controls us. The spirit that is at work in the people of the world no longer holds any power over our lives. This is graphically seen in various places in Scripture.

In Egypt when Moses was seeking to bring the children of Israel out from their bondage, God rained judgments down on the nation time and again. Yet, the people of God, and their families, their land, their businesses and their possessions were unaffected. The Israelites lived in the land of Goshen. This choice area had been gifted to them due to the favour on Joseph's life. Pharaoh had benefited so much from the guidance, wisdom, and oversight of Joseph, he rewarded him by giving his family some of the best land in Egypt. We are told that when the curses from God fell on the land, Goshen was spared.

"...but the Lord will make a distinction between the livestock of Israel and that of Egypt, so that no animal belonging to the Israelites will die." Exodus 9:4

"...and the next day the Lord did it: All the livestock of the Egyptians died, but not one animal belonging to the Israelites died." Exodus 9:6

"The only place it did not hail was the land of Goshen, where the Israelites were." Exodus 9:26

"No one could see anyone else or leave his place for three days. Yet all the Israelites had light in the places where they lived." Exodus 10:23

"...there will be loud wailing throughout Egypt--worse than there has ever been or ever will be again. But among the Israelites not a dog will bark at any man or animal. Then you will know that the Lord makes a distinction between Egypt and Israel." Exodus 11:6,7

"The blood will be a sign for you on the houses where you are; and when I see the blood, I will pass over you. No destructive plague will touch you when I strike Egypt." Exodus 12:13

The dreadful finale of these judgements was the death of all the firstborn throughout the land. Every Israelite household had been told to paint the blood of a slain lamb over the doorposts of their home. The angel of death bringing the plague of death to Egypt passed over the homes of God's people. Through the blood of the slain lamb each household was set free from the world and all the terror of its judgments.

In Genesis 26 Isaac remained in the land of Canaan, even though there was a famine in the land. He stayed because God told him to. He was to remain in the Promised Land. For us, this is remaining in Christ, just like the Israelites in Egypt remained in Goshen and avoided the plagues, so as we remain in Christ, we are set free from the curses that the world endures. This means we live in Christ, not in the world. We live in the ways of Christ; not the ways of the world. We become successful by honest means, not by cheating. We live like Christ; not like the world. We live separated to God; separate from the world. This is a position the devil would love us to compromise. He would seduce us away from the principles of Christ, having us believe that going the way of the world is the sure way to succeed. When we sacrifice our integrity to the god of success, we move out of Christ. This is what Isaac was tempted to do. He was warned to remain in the land. As he did this blessing came on his world.

> "**There was a famine in the land, besides the first famine that was in the days of Abraham. And Isaac went to Abimelech king of the Philistines, in Gerar. Then the Lord appeared to him and said: 'Do not go down to Egypt; live in the land of which I shall tell you. Dwell in this land, and I will be with you and bless you; for to you and your descendants I give all these lands, and I will perform the oath which I swore to Abraham your father'.**" Genesis 26:1-3

Isaac simply carried on normal farming activities. While the rest of the land was in famine, he prospered enormously. While all the fields around him were brown and barren, his were green and flourishing. All around him people were losing. He was winning.

> **"Then Isaac sowed in that land, and reaped in the same year a hundredfold; and the LORD blessed him.The man began to prosper, and continued prospering until he became very prosperous...for he had possessions of flocks and possessions of herds and a great number of servants. So the Philistines envied him."** Genesis 26:12-14

Noahs Ark is another very clear picture of God's people being set free from the world. Whatever calamity is coming on the world, we are able to escape it through being in Christ. All those who believed God and got into the ark were saved from the terrible disaster that covered the Earth.

It would seem as though there was no way whatsoever out of the flood. But God had called a man to prepare a way out. Those who accepted God's way were delivered; those who did not were drowned in the catastrophe.

Even though Lot was backslidden and had lost his way in God, he was still part of the covenant family. The covenant God had cut with Abraham extended to Lot and his family. When the judgment of God is finally about to fall upon Sodom and Gomorrah, angels from heaven come to rescue the man from the coming doom. Lot attempts to rescue his family also, but his witness has become so weak through a heavily compromised lifestyle, that he has no influence over his family. He is even hesitant about leaving the city he has fallen in love with. As they leave, they are warned not even to look back. However, Lot's wife pines for her life back in Sodom. She turns to watch as the city is destroyed. Lot and his daughters keep going. His wife turns to a pillar of salt. Remaining in Christ is staying free from the world. Christ gives us the power to separate from the world. As we remain focussed on Him we are set free from its enticements. It no longer chains us to either its pleasures or its pains.

God establishes the fact that His people are separated for the world through blessing as much as through the disasters they are protected from. God does wonders amongst His people that no other group on Earth experience.

> "**Then the Lord said: 'I am making a covenant with you. Before all your people I will do wonders never before done in any nation in all the world. The people you live among will see how awesome is the work that I, the Lord, will do for you.'**" Exodus 34:10

We don't have to accept the plagues that come on the Earth!

> "**A thousand may fall at your side, and ten thousand at your right hand; But it shall not come near you.**" Psalm 91:7

It is amazing how many Christians think that if disaster is happening in the world then it must be going to happen to them. If a financial recession comes upon the world we don't have to join it! **We are of another Kingdom than of this**

world. Our source of provision, and blessing is not this world. God will always find a way for us to be blessed even when the world is in trouble. God directed Elijah to the brook Cherith when Israel suffered famine (1Ki17:3). He commanded ravens to feed the prophet at the brook. This is a miraculous provision that He provided His servant. Elijah obeyed God and went exactly where God told him. When we go where we are commanded this is the same as remaining in Christ. The prophet received provision over the next three and a half years; first by ravens, then by a widow. Both were miraculous events. Ravens are one of the most selfish of creatures, unwilling to share anything they've discovered with another, yet their nature had been so altered by God that every morning and evening they brought food they had found to the man of God. After some time the brook Cherith dried up in the drought and Elijah received instruction to move on to a town called Zarephath where he was told a widow would provide for him. However, when Elijah arrived at Zarephath he discovered the widow was about to die from starvation. She had absolutely no food except for a handful of wheat. Elijah told her to give him the last of her food. She obeyed and this generosity triggered the release of abundance so that throughout the rest of the famine neither she, nor her family, nor the prophet went without. **God works through miraculous means to supply His people when the rest of the world is struggling.**

Being in Christ means we are set free from the world and all the curses that are sitting on it. Much of the time the Christian church has looked like it needed to be set free from itself. It has looked like the world is enjoying prosperity, having much more fun, and generally getting along a lot better than those in Christ. This thinking is from the devil.

If we imagine we are meant to be struggling through this life we are never going to be a great witness for Christ.

Yet many imagine it is godlier to be suffering the troubles of this age than to be living in victory! This is not just about reaching lost people for Christ either. This is about keeping those who have decided for Jesus, in the Kingdom. Many Christians become discouraged simply because they are labouring to get along in this life reasonably successfully, but are hamstrung by false concepts of what Christ is expecting of us. Many have been taught that prosperity is wrong, that holiness means being out of date and out of touch with this life, and that we have to commit intellectual suicide to follow Jesus. These concepts may be embraced for a brief time. But eventually the Christian discovers the incredible difficulties of living in the world whilst holding many of these wrong beliefs.

Much of Christian thinking is simply inherited culture. When the Christian community overlays its culture as though it is a requirement for holiness, then people are manipulated by guilt into a very uncomfortable lifestyle which plainly becomes impossible for them to live. They slip away from Christ, not realising **the standards they were trying to keep were not from the Lord in the first place.**

There are obviously things that are right and wrong as outlined in Scripture. But there is a also a whole world.

> **"You shall not be afraid of the terror by night, nor of the arrow that flies by day...nor of the pestilence that walks in darkness, nor of the destruction that lays waste at noonday...A**

thousand may fall at your side, and ten thousand at your right hand; but it shall not come near you...Only with your eyes shall you look, and see the reward of the wicked.

Because you have made the LORD, who is my refuge, even the Most High, your dwelling place...No evil shall befall you, nor shall any plague come near your dwelling...For He shall give His angels charge over you, to keep you in all your ways." Psalm 91:5-11

9

SPEAK THE WORD

"...it is written..."

9

SPEAK THE WORD

"God has not given to us a spirit of fear but of power, love, and a sound mind..."
2 Timothy 1:7

"Have faith in God..."
Mark 11:22

"...I am the LORD who heals you."
Exodus 15:26

"...He Himself took our infirmities and bore our sicknesses."
Matthew 8:17

"Whosoever shall say to this mountain be thou removed and cast into the sea and shall not doubt in his heart but shall believe that those things he says shall come to pass he shall have whatsoever he says..."
Mark 11:23

"What things soever you desire when you pray believe that you receive them and you shall have them..."
Mark 11:24

"Let us hold fast the profession of our faith without wavering for He who made the promise is faithful."
Hebrews 10:23

"Fear not for I have redeemed you. I have called you by your name, you are mine. When you pass through the waters I will be with you and when you pass through the rivers they will not overwhelm you. When you walk through the flames you will not be burned, the flames will not set you ablaze."
Isaiah 43:2

"...FEAR NOT FOR I AM WITH YOU..."
Isaiah 43:2

"My God shall supply all your need according to His riches in glory by Christ Jesus."
Philippians 4:19

"I can do all things through Christ who strengthens me..."
Philippians 4:13

"...with God all things are possible..."
Matthew 19:26

"Nothing is impossible to him who believes..." Luke 1:37

"Thanks be unto God who always causes us to triumph."
2 Corinthians 2:14

"God, calls those things which are not as though they were."
Romans 4:17

"Whatever you ask in my Name, that will I do."
John 14:13

"Ask and you shall receive, knock and it shall be opened to you, seek and you shall find..."
Matthew 7:7

"If you meditate in the words of this book...day and night...and do not let them depart from your mouth...then you will have good success."
Joshua 1:8

"If you abide in me and my words abide in you, you shall ask what you will and it shall be done unto you."
John 15:26

"If you ask me anything in My Name I will do it."
John 14:14

"He who meditates in the Word of God... whatsoever he does will prosper."
Psalm 1:3

"Now faith is the substance of things hoped for, the evidence of things not seen."
Hebrews 11:1

"All things you ask in prayer, believing you shall receive."
Matthew 21:22

"Beloved I wish above all things that you prosper and be in health even as your soul prospers."
3 John :2

"Whatever is born of God overcomes the world and this is the victory that overcomes the world, even our faith..."
1 John 5:4

"Greater is He that is in you than he that is in the world."
1 John 4:4

"No weapon that is formed against you shall prosper..."
Isaiah 54:17

"Fear not, you will not be put to shame, do not fear disgrace, you will not be humiliated."
Isaiah 54:4

"All your children will be taught by the Lord and great will be your children's peace."
Isaiah 54:13

"Be anxious for nothing, but in everything by prayer and supplication with thanksgiving make your requests known to God."
Philippians 4:6

"Cast all your burdens upon the Lord and He will sustain you."
Psalm 55:22

"Delight yourself in the Lord and He will give you the desires of your heart."
Psalm 37:3

"Commit your way to the Lord, trust in Him and He will do it."
Psalm 37:5

"All things are possible to him who believes."
Mark 9:23

**"All things work together for good
to those who love God
who are called according to his purpose."**
Romans 8:28

"I will never leave you or forsake you."
Hebrews 13:5

If you enjoyed
DEAD FOR NOTHING?
we would like to recommend the following
books by Dr Phil Pringle.

Faith
Moving In The Spirit And The Anointing
Healing The Wounded Spirit
You The Leader
Keys To Financial Excellence
The Leadership Files

Also by Chris Pringle.

Jesse – Found In Heaven

For more information please write to:

PaX Ministries Pty Ltd
Locked Bag 8, Dee Why NSW 2099 AUSTRALIA
Email: pax@ccc.org.au

or visit the Pax website at
www.ccc.org.au/pax

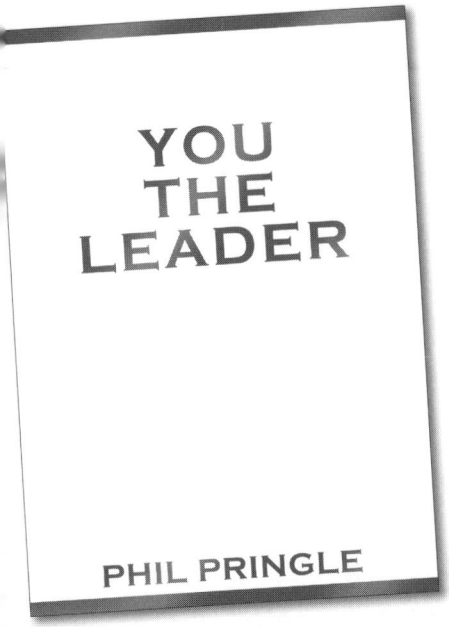

What people are saying about "You The Leader" by Dr Phil Pringle

"I would like to recommend 'You the Leader' by Dr. Phil Pringle. All true Christians are called to use their talents and gifts in a position of authority in the Body of Christ. This book will help each Christian understand his or her role in the Body of Christ."

Dr. David Yonggi Cho
The Yoido Full Gospel Church, Seoul, Korea

"Phil Pringle is an apostolic leader par-excellence. He is also one of the few leaders who knows how to mentor others and to communicate what he knows. 'You The Leader', is crammed full of extraordinary insights that will help you become the dynamic leader that God wants you to be! I highly recommend it."

C. Peter Wagner, Chancellor
Chancellor, Wagner Leadership Institute, USA

"'You The Leader' is a must read for any person who feels called to leadership in the body of Christ. Dr Pringle's insight, gained from over 30 years of pastoral ministry, is practical, biblically based and includes thinking in the area of leadership that I believe to be revolutionary in the contemporary church"

Joyce Meyer
Joyce Meyer Ministries, St. Louis, USA

To order these or any other books by Dr Phil Pringle, log on to the PaX website at www.ccc.org.au

GAIN...

Enthusiasm, opportunity, significance, focus, success, passion, patience, wisdom...

DEAL WITH...

Discouragement, culture, people, attitudes, criticism, unfinished business, guilt, confrontation...

'THE LEADERSHIP FILES' is a compilation of notes to YOU the LEADER, giving you quick, practical, encouraging and inspiring messages that will assist you in the day-to-day issues of life and leadership.

Your world will transform as you apply these to your daily life.

SUBSCRIBE NOW! LEADERSHIP FILES ONLINE

Sign up now to receive Ps Phil Pringle's 'Leadership Files' – a weekly injection o inspiration for you and your leadership team, straight to your inbox!
Simply log on to www.ccc.org.au and follow the links!

Find the Keys To Financial Excellence!

If we are to achieve the purposes that God has for the church in this world, it is imperative that we have a liberal and bountiful attitude about money and giving, where the abundance of heaven can freely flow.

Join Phil Pringle as he steps boldly and unapologetically into the fullness of what the Word of God has to say about money, prosperity and the power of giving.

"*'Keys To Financial Excellence' is real help for real people wanting wisdom in a world of conflicting messages about something as fundamental and profound as their money.*"

John C. Maxwell *Founder, The INJOY Group.*
www.INJOY.com

To order this or any other books by Dr Phil Pringle, log on to the PaX website at www.ccc.org.au

There is no doubt that it is the men and women of faith who have changed the world

God has dealt to every man, woman and child a measure of faith.

Discover the "aliveness" of the God of all creation and be one of this uncommon breed of people who transform this world by faith.

PaX

To order this or any other books by Dr Phil Pringle, log on to the PaX website at www.ccc.org.au

"Safe in angels arms, far from here, our children run and play..."

Jesse...Found in Heaven" will bring hope and comfort to every family suffering the loss of a baby or child.

"*What a beautiful treasure this book has been in my life and the lives of those I have shared it with. 'Jesse – Found In Heaven' has touched a place deep in my heart personally and has created a greater anticipation for the wonder and beauty of what we will encounter when we are reunited with our little loved ones in Heaven. What joy!*"

Helen Burns
Senior Pastor Victory Christian Centre, Vancouver BC
TV Presenter "Pure Sex and Relationships" CH 10 Vancouver BC

Video and Audio CD also available.

Chris Pringle is the 'first lady' of Christian City Church Oxford Falls, Sydney, having founded the CCC movement with her husband Phil in 1980. A refreshing voice on the scene of Christendom, Chris has refused to tread the weary path that tends to pigeon hole, and therefore diminish, the value and effectiveness of women in church life. As preacher, pastor, and leader, Chris combines wisdom, insight, humour and the ability to go where angels fear to tread!

PAXMinistries

Available at your favourite Christian retailer or online at www.ccceshop.com.au